The state of the art

Teaching drama in the 21st century

Edited by Michael Anderson and
Colleen Roche

SYDNEY UNIVERSITY PRESS

First published in 2015 by Sydney University Press
© Individual contributors 2015
© Sydney University Press 2015

Reproduction and Communication for other purposes
Except as permitted under the Act, no part of this edition may be reproduced, stored in a retrieval system, or communicated in any form or by any means without prior written permission. All requests for reproduction or communication should be made to Sydney University Press at the address below:

Sydney University Press
Fisher Library F03
University of Sydney NSW 2006
AUSTRALIA
Email: sup.info@sydney.edu.au
sydney.edu.au/sup

National Library of Australia Cataloguing-in-Publication Data

Title:	State of the art : teaching drama in the 21st century / edited by Michael Anderson and Colleen Roche.
ISBN:	9781743320273 (paperback)
ISBN:	9781743320280 (ebook : epub)
Notes:	Includes bibliographical references and index.
Subjects:	Drama in education--New South Wales
	Drama -- Study and teaching -- New South Wales.
	Improvisation (Acting) -- Study and teaching--New South Wales.
	Theater -- Study and teaching -- New South Wales.
Other Authors/ Contributors:	Anderson Michael 1969-, editor.
	Roche, Colleen, editor.
Dewey Number:	792.028

Cover image: detail of Plate 1: Waratah (*Telopea speciosissima*, R. Br.) from JH Maiden. *The flowering plants and ferns of New South Wales.* Sydney: Charles Potter, Government Printer, 1895.

Cover design by Miguel Yamin.

Contents

Foreword v

Introduction ix

1 The power of drama pedagogy and research to open doors: dwelling in the house of possibility
 Miranda Jefferson 1

2 School drama: towards state of the art in drama professional learning?
 Robyn Ewing, Robyn Gibson, Victoria Campbell, John Saunders and Helen Hristofski 25

3 Drama and ecological understanding: stories of learning
 David Wright 49

4 Schooling the imagination in the 21st century . . . (or why playbuilding matters)
 Christine Hatton and Sarah Lovesy 67

5 Learning English as an additional language (EAL) through the pedagogy of educational drama
 Margery Hertzberg 85

6	What's wrong with the way we teach playwriting? *Paul Gardiner*	109
7	The drama of co-intentional dialogue: reflections on the confluent praxis of Dorothy Heathcote and Paulo Freire *Gerard Boland*	129
8	Hold the phone: drama education and mobile technology *David Cameron and Rebecca Wotzko*	149

About the contributors   171

Index   177

Foreword

It's been 10 years since the last edition in this series, making it all the more welcome. *The state of the art* is a powerful frame through which to make sense of the unfolding turbulent flow of drama education in the wider stream of Australian and international arts education.

As the earlier publications (Hughes 1991; Michaels 1994; Hatton & Anderson 2004) remind us, drama education is anything but 'steady state' where constants are maintained in cosmic suspension. Drama education is an expanding universe. It operates within a dynamic push–pull flow of ideas and practice.

Australian arts education and drama education in 2015 is poised at yet another tipping point. As Anderson and Roche comment in their introduction, there are anxieties, challenges and the need for re-balancing. The lengthy development period for the *Australian curriculum: the arts* (2014) – and the even more protracted and troubled implementation of this curriculum – remind us that Australian education has been here before. Our current curriculum policy is inscribed on a palimpsest of past arts curriculum development. It is the plaything of politics and competing forces. There is reason for concern about the realisation of an enduring arts curriculum with full recognition of drama. As John O'Toole sketched in his foreword to the 2004 *State of our art*, on the one hand, the development of drama education has arisen from 'a community … [that] gives and receives the gifts of good practice generously' (v). But he also notes, tentatively, the need to 'position drama within the dominant discourses of education' (viii).

It is worth asking in 2015 if that caution has been turned to confidence. Has drama education found a secure place in dominant educational discourse?

A climate of uncertainty for implementing Australian arts curriculum reinforces the value of this series of books as markers of time and action in Australian drama education. The initiative of the Educational Drama Association of New South Wales (now Drama NSW) is assisting us to understand better where we are now and where we might go in the future. Bill Green (2003) reminds us of the necessity of understanding the genealogy of curriculum at a local level. The stories shared in this book resonate beyond their immediate setting and have value for the wider arts and drama community, not just in Australia.

The state of the art (2015) positions drama education in the crucible of debate about 21st-century skills: critical thinking and problem solving, collaboration, networking, creative thinking, capacity building, metaphoric thinking and cognitive playfulness (to point to a few). This publication theorises drama education practice within a vibrant research culture and asserts drama as something more than 'curriculum tricks' or teacher 'time-fillers'.

Miranda Jefferson highlights the essential 'givens' of drama pedagogy – deep, scaffolded creative and critical thinking, and empathy (themes taken up by many of the writers in the book). These givens powerfully resonate with capacity to socialise learning through community and agency, activating oracy and language, and envisioning and rehearsing alternatives. In her chapter, and throughout the other chapters, there is strongly situated advocacy for the value and place of drama education. Underpinning the arguments made throughout the book is a commitment to sound research and scholarship grounded in rigorous understanding of practice.

Interwoven through the book are the challenges of implementing disruptive pedagogies and resistance to them. Within the broad optimism of Jefferson's 'dwelling in the house of possibility' there are the reminders of difficulties and issues. This book celebrates the possible breadth of drama education: in literacy, partnerships, English as an additional language, ecological understandings, schooling the imagination, playwriting, co-intentional dialogues and technology. This book

Foreword

reflects the vaulting ambition and vision of drama education. Yet it does not skirt the issues. Ewing, Gibson, Campbell and Hristofski point to primary teachers' lack of expertise and confidence. They argue for the value of opening drama beyond the conventional confines of the classroom and embracing quality partnerships and teaching artists, engaging with literature and story. David Wright envisages a role for drama in broader ecological frameworks and conflicts. David Cameron and Rebecca Wotzko share a passion for the power of increasingly ever-present technologies in drama and the challenges they bring. Margery Hertzberg takes us into the sphere of drama in English as an additional language. Hatton and Lovesy craft the case for improvisation and play building. Paul Gardiner focuses on teaching and learning of playwriting. Gerard Boland makes connections between Heathcote and Freire and models of quality teaching.

While *The state of the art* reminds us of the gaps, it also highlights possibilities. To focus on the state of the any art is to reflect on the highest level of development at a particular moment in time and place. This collection powerfully meets that challenge.

Another welcome strength of this book is the respectful acknowledgment of the drama education community's pioneers and leaders: John Carroll, Dorothy Heathcote and many more. We are what are today as an arts and drama education community because we are communities of shared practice and research, critically, creatively and collaboratively engaged with each other. It is equally encouraging that there are new voices. Our drama education universe is ever expanding.

In his *Making mirrors* (2001) album Gotye's song 'State of the art' urges us:

State, state, state, state of the art (Listen to the difference!)
State, state, state, state of the art (It is time to hear the results)

I urge you to read this *State of the art*, listening to the difference and hearing the results. Enjoy the state of the art. Make the most of the drama that's been made but also look forward to the next time we take the pulse of Australian drama education.

Robin Pascoe
Perth, March 2015

Works cited

Green B (2003). Curriculum inquiry in Australia: toward a local genealogy of the curriculum field. In W Pinar (Ed). *International handbook of curriculum research* (pp123-41). Mahwah, NJ: L. Erlbaum Associates.

Michaels W (Ed) (1993). *Drama in education: the state of the art II*. Leichhardt, NSW: Educational Drama Association.

Hatton C & M Anderson M (Eds). *The state of our art: NSW perspectives on educational drama*. Sydney: Currency Press; Educational Drama Association of New South Wales.

Hughes J (1991). *Drama in education: the state of the art, an Australian perspective*. Rozelle, NSW: Educational Drama Association.

O'Toole J (2004). Foreword. In C Hatton & M Anderson (Eds). *The state of our art: NSW perspectives on educational drama*. Sydney: Currency Press; Educational Drama Association of New South Wales.

Introduction

When we were kids we loved to collect 'best of' albums. They were usually called things like 'Ripper Tracks 1989' or '1982 with a Bullet'. They were a kind of grab bag of hits from that year which demonstrated what music had been and to some extent what popular music would become. In some ways the 'State of the art' series is similar. It is a showcase of where we have been, where we are and where we might be coming to. The series has played an important role as a focal point for practitioners and researchers in drama education in New South Wales and beyond. Through this series, the NSW drama community has celebrated research and scholarship from generations of drama education researchers. *State of the art* continues to reflect a diverse range of interests and preoccupations. The contributors to this volume also mirror the changes in curriculum and approach that drama education has seen since the last edition, *The state of our art: NSW perspectives in educational drama*, almost a decade ago. Before we discuss the specifics of the contributions to this volume it may be worth considering some of the shifts that have occurred in drama education in the last 10 years.

The shift in policy by the Rudd and Gillard governments towards a national curriculum stirred some excitement in the arts education com-

Anderson M & Roche C (2015). Introduction. In M Anderson & C Roche (Eds). *The state of the art: teaching drama in the 21st century*, (ix–xii). Sydney: Sydney University Press.

munity. The inclusion of the arts, comprising dance, drama, media arts, music and visual arts, in the second phase of curriculum development was felt to be a bit of a coup, but more likely was a necessary and important acknowledgement of the place of the arts in Australian schools. In many ways, the process has tipped off a predictable curriculum turf war between those who wish to see the old hierarchy of music and visual arts as primary and the 'other' art forms left to pick up what time is left. The Australian curriculum does however offer the arts education community the opportunity for a rebalancing of this situation and for art forms to get equal access to arts opportunities. There are, in some quarters, anxieties about what these changes mean for arts in schools but these challenges aren't new. The challenges of curriculum change have been an ever-present feature of the schooling landscape and will probably continue to be so. Some of the approaches and ideas contained in this volume lead the way in understanding how curriculum innovation can support the growth of drama as a school subject in the face of ever-present curriculum change.

This collection also marks the growth of a research culture in schools and universities. Many of the authors featured here are new to the research scene but experienced classroom teachers who have been leaders in curriculum and assessment over the years. Their contribution in this volume, and in other places, has been to revitalise and renew the link between schools and universities to create a strong partnership for describing, analysing and reflecting on learning in drama.

The collection opens with Miranda Jefferson's discussion of the process of researching in the arts. Her article poetically tracks her personal discoveries through her evolving understanding of drama, pedagogy and broader issues in student learning. In chapter 2 'School drama: towards state of the art in drama professional learning?' Robyn Ewing, Robyn Gibson, Victoria Campbell and Helen Hristofski revisit a theme that has exercised the minds and hearts of many of the contributors to the 'State of the art' series. Their reflections on the innovative school drama process not only have implications for drama learning, but also engage in active discussions of learning across the curriculum. David Wright considers the ways drama can provoke understanding in other fields. He argues in his conclusion that 'drama education can be seen as a laboratory for the ongoing exploration of participation in unfolding awareness'. His reflections will support those looking for ways

Introduction

to enhance learning about our fragile and changing world. In chapter 4 Christine Hatton and Sarah Lovesy remind us of the centrality of playbuilding in learning. Their discussion explores the way many drama processes align directly with 21st-century learning approaches. Margery Hertzberg's chapter, 'Learning English as an Additional Language (EAL) through educational drama' examines an area that has been extensively researched in recent times. Hertzberg unpacks the opportunities and challenges for drama and EAL in a way that will be directly relevant to classroom learning. Paul Gardiner's chapter, 'What's wrong with the way we teach playwriting?' provokes the reader through a discussion of what is currently working and not working about playwriting in NSW schools. His reflections introduce the opportunity for improved practice in an area that is the heart and soul of theatre and drama education. Jerry Boland's chapter, 'The drama of co-intentional dialogue: reflections on the confluent praxis of Dorothy Heathcote and Paulo Freire' celebrates the practices of these pioneering educational figures and considers their application in drama classrooms. His discussion will be relevant to teachers interested in creating democratic engaged learners. The volume concludes with 'Hold the phone: drama education and mobile technology' by David Cameron and Rebecca Wotzko. This chapter reminds us of the affordances and relevance of emergent technologies to drama learning and helps us to reflect on what might be in the drama classroom as well as what currently is.

This volume of *State of the art* represents some of the best aspects of drama education in NSW. The work is rigorous and grounded in an understanding and experience of classroom practice. The chapters reflect the aspirational nature of drama education to broadly influence learning. These chapters extend drama education beyond curriculum boundaries into many aspects of young people's lives. Finally the work honours and reflects the rich tradition of classroom-based research of pioneers such as John Carroll and Dorothy Heathcote. John's influence over the work in this series has been profound and many of the contributors represented here (ourselves included) owe him a debt of gratitude. In many ways the fruits of his legacy can be seen in the fertility and growth of practice and research in drama.

Many challenges lie ahead but there is much to be optimistic about in these pages. The partnerships evident in this volume and indeed this series suggest drama education in NSW has not only a strong history, but also a bright future.

Michael Anderson
Colleen Roche

1
The power of drama pedagogy and research to open doors: dwelling in the house of possibility

Miranda Jefferson

> I dwell in Possibility –?
> A fairer House than Prose –
> More numerous of Windows –
> Superior – for Doors –
> *Emily Dickenson, 1862*

Dwelling in possibility for Emily Dickenson is dwelling in the metaphoric house of aesthetic freedom where she can create the emotional, intellectual and spiritual dimensions of experience through the limitless possibilities of poetry. For me, 'dwelling in possibility' is imagining and using the force and potential of drama as a process of learning. Dickenson's poem also encapsulates the windows and doors that PhD research has opened for me in terms of possibilities. This chapter is about the power of the research journey and drama pedagogy to open doors for both students and teachers to explore their learning capacity and potential.

My research journey is the 'backstory' of this chapter. As a backstory it explains the context in which I find myself. The backstory is significant because it gives value to the process of research and ex-

---

Jefferson M (2015). The power of drama pedagogy and research to open doors: dwelling in the house of possibility. In M Anderson & C Roche (Eds). *The state of the art: teaching drama in the 21st century,* (1–23). Sydney: Sydney University Press.

plains how the product or outcomes of the research have been formed to frame and construct the post-research 'fore story'. The fore story is the drama literacy and teacher capacity-building program I am currently running in primary schools. Communicating and connecting the backstory and fore story serve to extrapolate how research is an ongoing narrative. It is a narrative that illustrates how research and drama pedagogy can contribute to innovation and the ongoing development of quality learning programs and outcomes for students and teachers. It is a story about engaging with pedagogy.

Research as an ongoing narrative

My PhD research (Jefferson 2011) was about drama, film and teaching. Inherent to these art forms and in many ways to learning is the act of storytelling. Stories make sense of our experience of the world. Experience is temporal and the telling and understanding of experience involves a selective emphasis of the experience (Dewey 1958). Choices and consequences of choices shape our lived experience, and the representation of those choices over time become stories (Bruner 1987). Stories not only make sense of our own lives and our experience, but the telling of stories are the means by which we can experience others' experience (Clandinin & Connelly 1994).

Narrative is retrospective meaning-making – the shaping or ordering of past experience. Narrative is a way of understanding one's own and others actions, of organising events and objects into a meaningful whole, and of connecting and seeing the consequences of actions and events over time (Chase 2008, 64).

In life and learning, storytelling opens windows of perception and understanding. In this chapter I use the structure of a story to organise and communicate my experience with research and drama pedagogy. I have constructed two narratives in the story pattern of a seven-part film narrative schema.[1] The chapter is not about the possibilities of two par-

---

1 Branigan in *Narrative comprehension and film* (1992) explains that a schema is a type of mental structure. A narrative schema is only one of many types of schema that can be applied to data to solve everyday problems. He asserts that nearly all researchers agree that the narrative schema has the following format: 1.

allel stories as in the movie *Sliding doors* (Dir. Howitt 1998); it is about connecting two stories. The first story is about research and the second about opportunities to implement ideas arising from that research. The stories are about the possibilities of effective and sustainable innovation in schools through research, drama and quality professional learning.

My backstory in research begins according to the narrative schema with a 'setting' and a 'character'. It also begins with the opening of two doors.

Opening doors: research beginnings (1. Introduction of setting and character)

I am the protagonist of this story, and the backstory begins with me working as a drama and film teacher in the setting of a NSW performing arts high school. After teaching a drama class and closing the door to the classroom I crossed the hallway and opened a door to another classroom to teach film. In the hallway I experienced a sense of metamorphosis, evolving from drama teacher into film teacher, and in that moment I asked the Kafkaesque question, 'What's happened to me?'

At the same time, I wasn't completely transformed, so the question, 'What has not happened to me?' was equally relevant. It was in the tension between being a film teacher and a drama teacher that my research journey began. Research is 'a systematic attempt to re-see the everyday' (Freebody 2003) and it was in the moment of metamorphosis that I wanted to understand and explore the newly emerging area of filmmaking in schools through the experiences of drama teachers.

The broader setting for the research story is the curriculum context of the state of NSW. This context does not determine the outcomes of the research but it does identify the conditions from which issues arise (Corbin & Strauss 2008). In drama these conditions are called the 'given circumstances'. In film narratives they are the 'state of affairs' and they contextualise the ongoing events of this research story.

---

introduction of setting and characters; 2. explanations of a state of affairs; 3. intitating event; 4. emotional response or statement of a goal by the protagonist; 5. complicating actions; 6. outcome; 7. reactions to the outcome.

Drama and film in NSW (2. Explanation of a state of affairs)

When I was teaching film from 2001 to 2005, filmmaking in schools was still a relatively new and uncertain area. In NSW it was explored in a piecemeal fashion and in different ways across curriculum areas such as English, visual arts, drama, and design and technology. At the performing arts high school where I was teaching we introduced a film course from years 9 to 12. This was in response to student interest, the accessibility and affordability of user-friendly camera and editing software, and as a response to the rapidly digitised and mediated world. The course was endorsed by the state curriculum authority, the NSW Board of Studies, and was immediately popular with students.

The introduction of information and communication technology (ICT) in schools at the time was compared to a 'hammer in search of a nail'. This describes the phenomenon where the implementation of technology is 'contrived or incongruent with classroom practice and discipline-specific pedagogy' (Hofer & Owings-Swan 2005, 102). Drama teachers interested in filmmaking were unsure how to develop pedagogy for effective learning with the new digital technology. They were 'in search of a nail'.

From this state of affairs a 'critical moment' or 'initiating event' in the narrative occurred.

A book and a case study (3. Initiating event)

The initiating event in the narrative was Michael Anderson from the University of Sydney asking me to co-write a book about the theory and practice of film pedagogy (Anderson & Jefferson 2009). He also encouraged me to do a PhD in this newly emerging and developing area of the curriculum. As an experienced drama teacher at a performing arts high school I had the opportunity to teach film as a discrete subject. This was unusual within the curriculum structures of most schools in NSW at the time. I was uniquely positioned to consider the aesthetics and pedagogy of film-learning possibilities from a drama-learning perspective. Our book explored filmmaking through an interdependent and recursive arts pedagogical model in making and appreciating.

Separate but related to the book, my PhD research was grounded in interpreting the real world experiences (Greenwood & Levin 2008) of drama teachers with film. It involved a case study of six drama teachers who, with other teachers, participated in an intervention of 36 hours of film pedagogy workshops that I facilitated. The aim of the case study was to provide a rich, detailed and close portrait of drama teachers and their film-learning experiences in the workshops and in their schools.

Case study research focuses on the particular or an instance, and attempts to gain theoretical and professional insights from a full documentation of that instance (Freebody 2003). The focus on the instance also reflects the universal, a connection made by Jean-Paul Sartre: 'a man is never an individual; it would be more fitting to call him a universal singular. Summed up and for this reason universalised by his epoch, he in turn resumes it by reproducing himself in its singularity' (1981, ix). To study the particular then is also to study the universal.

The strength of a collective case study is to explore a phenomenon that leads to better understanding and perhaps better theorising about a larger collection of cases (Stake 2008). The benefit of a case study in education is to use localised experience in order to appreciate and integrate the complexity and uniqueness of practice, and to avoid theorising 'in a vacuum' (Freebody 2003).

Undertaking research however requires the researcher to have motivation or objective to catapult the research process forward. For me the motivation was to make a difference.

Making a difference (4. Emotional response or statement of goal by the protagonist)

The emotional response to undertaking a book and PhD as a first-time experience was excitement at the challenge but incredulity that I made such a decision. It is however the statement of a goal that ultimately drives the researcher and the research narrative forward. I had the curiosity to gain personal knowledge through research but I was also passionate about developing what I saw as the effectiveness and benefits of drama and film in many young people's learning experiences. I wanted to make a difference by contributing to the professional learning of the teachers participating in my research and more broadly to the policy and practice of arts learning in NSW.

Such goals are perhaps fanciful but I found my research aspirations in the words of Peter Freebody (2003). He describes research in education as a 'discourse of cultural optimism' that aims to 'change the social world by discovering better understandings of its qualities' (218). It was this sense of optimism and idealism to make a difference that set me on the research path. But despite aspirational goals and intentions to change the 'social world', research like a story is never without the cause and effect of unforeseen events or complicating actions to upset those goals.

Unforeseen events in research (5. Complicating actions)

In a film narrative complicating actions are obstacles in the way of attaining a goal. In research complicating actions are often unplanned events. A case study is described as a 'naturalistic-experiment-in action' (Freebody 2003) but unforeseen events are at first considered a derailment of a well-thought-through research design. An unforeseen event during my PhD occurred after I had collected my research data. It was the development of the Australian curriculum, and the draft 'Arts shape' paper in 2010. The national curriculum for the arts was to include five subjects: dance, drama, media arts, music and visual arts. The inclusion and possibilities of the new subject media arts changed the 'state of affairs' for my research narrative. It re-oriented my discussion of how drama teachers in NSW could integrate and innovate a pedagogical approach to film.

The changing 'given circumstances' of a national curriculum set about a chain of events of another post-research 'fore story' about media arts. But that post-research story is a chapter for another book. Complications such as unplanned events in research do however create a fresh perspective on the research data and highlight how unforeseen problems and challenges are further possibilities for knowledge. In this case, it was how an aesthetic experiential pedagogical approach to film could be accommodated in a changing curriculum landscape. As the 'social world' of education was changing around me different paradigms and narratives in curriculum construction (Pinar et al. 1995; Ewing 2010) arose as a tension and issue in the research analysis.

Another 'complicating factor' or 'obstacle' in the research was the unexpected emergence of teachers' professional learning as a theme in the data. As the interviews, questionnaires and reflective logbook data was gathered and codified, the nature of teacher professional learning became meaningful as a pattern across the collective case study analysis (Patton 2002). The original focus of the research was about drama teachers and film but the interventionist film workshops made the nature and effectiveness of teacher professional learning a significant area of focused study.

The unexpected events in national curriculum development and the unforeseen data in teacher professional learning were 'complications' that enriched the study and contributed significantly to the research narrative. Complications serve to demonstrate how the open and challenging process of analysis in research can lead to the discovery of possibilities and new meanings in knowledge. The ultimate findings of the PhD were highly influenced by these unforeseen and complicating factors. Complicating actions in a narrative lead to an outcome, and in a research narrative these are the conclusions or findings.

Findings from the research (6. Outcome)

The 'outcome' of a narrative is the climax and resolution that ends the conflict. The obstacles preventing the protagonist to attain their goal are overcome. Complicating actions are obstacles in PhD research but writing up a PhD is in itself an obstacle. A PhD is a monolith, a mountain and a millstone that has to be overcome and conquered. Sheer tenacity is the only way to resolve the 'conflict' of completing it. The climax in the research narrative is successfully submitting the PhD. In terms of attaining goals I had explored and analysed the problematised areas of film and drama, technology and pedagogy, and innovation in professional learning and curriculum development.

Imperative to me was empowering the teachers involved in the research and so underpinning the research was the collaborative, participatory and transformative orientation of critical theory (Freire 2006 [1970]; Kincheloe & McLaren 2005). I had aimed to empower the research participants to reflect upon and understand their own situation and support future action in their teaching and learning of film and drama. As the data shows, the research did have a positive and transforming impact on the professional learning of the teachers involved in the project. However my goal to 'make a difference' beyond the research process wasn't realised. It became a motivation for the ensuing fore story.

The outcome of the research was the recommendations based on the collective case study. These conclusions were 'naturalistic generalisations' (Stake 1978) made from the detailed and rich analysis of six drama teachers and their experiences. The six teachers' reflections suggested that the creative and experiential pedagogical processes of the research workshops contributed to dynamic and transformative professional learning. An implication of the research was that teachers are empowered by professional learning that is characterised by experiential, creative and collaborative processes (Moran & John-Steiner 2003) and ongoing action learning with an academic partner (Aubusson et al. 2009).

The 36 hours of film pedagogy workshops created a vibrant professional learning community modeled on the shared understanding and participation of a 'community of practice' (Lave & Wenger 1991). Teachers with a mutual interest in film and drama, and with shared problems and challenges came together to share, reflect on and develop professional practice through creative and critical learning processes. As the researcher mentor I was able to facilitate and support action learning processes in reflection, community, action and feedback. Solving problems through action and learning by the people who face the problems is the ethos of action learning (Revans 1980). The group's sharing experiences, and supporting and challenging each other to take action and to learn 'implies both organization development and self-development – action on a problem that changes both the problem and the actor' (Pedler 1996, xxx). Hargreaves (2003, 25) argues that, 'Not one teacher knows enough to cope or improve by ?himself or herself. It is vital that teachers engage in action, inquiry, and problem-solving together in collegial teams or professional learning communities'.

Throughout and after the workshops the teachers reflected together about their own learning and the learning of their students, and solved issues about how to innovate and develop film in their schools. For the teachers the intensive and experiential workshops were a unique and stimulating experience that developed confidence, motivation and a more positive yet critical approach to teaching generally. The teachers' reflections in the research suggested opportunities for establishing effective and ongoing professional learning communities in NSW. Such communities are not widely accessible, sustained or inherent in the current systemic and school structures. Unfortunately, I was unable to continue with the teachers as a professional 'community of learners' (Brown 2005) due to my focus on analysing and writing up the study, and a lack of resources to support such an idea. To make a difference by supporting the capacity-building of teachers through processes informed by my research was an idea that came to fruition later in the 'fore story'.

Another recommendation from the research was the need to develop deep and scaffolded, creative and critical learning in the aesthetic of film within the curriculum context of the new Australian arts curriculum and the subject of media arts. For the drama teachers in the research project, learning through the making and appreciating of film had the capacity to create a rich and complex, challenging and authentic learning experience for students. The teachers observed that effective film learning used creative and collaborative learning processes, experiential and performative processes of learning, and narrative and performative codes of representation for an audience. These ideas seemed specific to the pedagogy of drama and film at the time but in my post-research journey, they resonated with broader concerns and possibilities in learning.

The findings in the PhD research are not the end of the story. The research narrative ends with an epilogue.

An epilogue in research (7. Reactions to the outcome)

According to Branigan (1992) the seventh and last component of the narrative schema is 'reactions to the outcome' or an epilogue. An epilogue is the moral lesson implicit in the events of the narrative or the lesson made explicit by the character's reactions to the narrative's resolution. My reaction was relief that the PhD was over, but also an uneasy sense that it wasn't. I did not feel I had put my research findings into practice. I had not fulfilled my goal of making a difference.

Research is an ongoing narrative. The 'findings' of my PhD have continued to evolve well beyond the finished thesis. The PhD research continues to be synthesised and analysed in light of the life experiences I continue to have. The door didn't close with the research but has remained open to further outcomes that continue to play out. This is where the research as a backstory connects to the fore story of this chapter. The fore story is about the consequences of research and the possibilities of drama pedagogy as future action in the classroom.

Opening doors: research as future action (1. Introduction of settings and characters)

The fore story begins again with the introduction of setting and character. I continue to be the protagonist but at the beginning of this story I am a teacher with a PhD lecturing part time at the University of Sydney. Like Pirandello's *Six characters in search of an author* I search for a role and place to apply my PhD learning and findings. My 'setting' is a psychological space shaped by the uncertainty that the all-consuming PhD research had not been realised more broadly in an ongoing sense in the real world. I felt the doors had closed and no longer felt I was 'dwelling in possibility'. Was I naïve to think that my research could make a difference?

Sixties' singer Peggy Lee's rendition of 'Is that all there is?' (Leiber & Stoller) and its lyrics of disillusionment were resonating in my head. But another maxim was also residing in my head: 'Drama bridges the conversation between our inner selves and the outside world' (Saxton & Miller 2009; Hughes 1991). Could drama be the conduit between my inner research learning self and real life actions in the outside world? The answer lies in the subsequent events of this story. These events are shaped by the state of affairs in the outside world. The state of affairs begins with the state of drama in NSW schools.

1 The power of drama pedagogy

The state of drama in schools (2. State of affairs)

Drama has grown as a subject in the secondary curriculum in NSW since the development of Board of Studies syllabi in 1986 and 1991, and in the primary curriculum in 2000. Despite its emergence in the curriculum and the recognition that drama is a pedagogy that promotes the development of multiliteracies, creativity, critical thinking, empathy and collaborative work practices drama still lies in the fringes of education with other arts subjects.

In primary schools drama is rarely core learning, nor is it utilised as a widespread pedagogy in other areas of the curriculum. Despite teaching practitioners and academics extolling the virtues of drama as a pedagogy in English (Anderson, Hughes & Manuel 2008; Neelands1992) and primary researchers and practitioners setting up programs using drama as literacy learning (Ewing & Simons 2004; Miller & Saxton 2004), drama and the arts more generally are still on the educational margins. O'Toole and Stinson's (2009) description of drama in education as clinging and 'unregarded but limpet-like out there beyond the mainstream' is the current state of affairs in NSW. Drama is not central to the curriculum and not core pedagogy.

But O'Toole and Stinson also point out that it is in the liminal space of the fringes where change agents can be found. It is in this liminal space where an 'initiating event' gave me an opportunity to be a change agent and make a difference.

Taking and making opportunities: drama and literacy (3. Initiating event)

In the uncertain setting of what to do post-PhD I was asked by Mark Hopkins at the Parramatta diocese Catholic Education Office (CEO) to be a critical friend for a drama and literacy program that had just been implemented in a few primary and secondary schools in Western Sydney. Mark was interested in my PhD research and the possibilities for developing arts pedagogy in primary schools, and developing the arts more generally in schools across an extensive diocese stretching from Parramatta to the Blue Mountains. The other issue to consider was developing literacy learning in these schools. It is in this initiating event that a 'door to possibility' had been opened.

The drama and literacy program had run only for two terms and involved a theatre artist, year 5 students and their teachers. The teaching theatre artist visited the primary classes once a week and explored a picture book through the pedagogy and aesthetic of drama. Linked to the drama classes were other literacy tasks to be explored by the primary classroom teacher. At a nearby secondary school the same theatre artist developed with secondary students a devised performance piece from the picture book. The devised work was then performed for the primary schools that had explored the same text through the drama and literacy program. The aim of the program was to improve students' literacy and encourage teachers to use drama as an experiential and kinaesthetic pedagogy.

Exploring picture books through drama and then connecting those explorations with other aspects of literacy has been investigated and instigated by seminal educational practitioners (e.g. Ewing & Simons 2004; Gibson & Ewing 2011; Miller & Saxton 2004; O'Toole & Dunn 2002). Through drama processes students embody the story's language, images and ideas. In enactment they combine affective and cognitive understandings, and by being actors and audience they make critical connections through reflection and analysis. It is literacy in three dimensions. Learning through picture books and drama provides 'spaces' and 'places' for the imagination to explore issues and feelings through metaphor and multiple perspectives (Saxton & Miller 2013).

In the age of communication and social connectivity through the internet there is an imperative for students to interrogate multimodal texts[2] beyond surface understandings. Exploring the text and images of picture books through drama has the capacity to develop learning in multimodal literacy, literary understandings, aesthetic experiences and critical literacies[3] as well as fostering students' imagination and creativity (Ewing et al. 2008). Drama as an experiential and kinaesthetic

---

2 Multimodal describes texts that combine two or more semiotic systems such as linguistic, visual, audio, gestural and spatial. Multimodal texts are delivered through different media; they may be live, paper, or digital.
3 Critical literacy is to examine texts as a sociological analysis. Originating from the work of Freire (2000 [1970]) critical literacy is to decode and construct

process provides an alternative way of learning for students often excluded by other teaching methods. Drama therefore supports functional literacy, as well as provides opportunities for empathetic engagement and a deeper understanding of texts and ideas (Belliveau & Prendergast 2013; Dunn et al. 2013; Ewing 2009; O'Mara 2008; O'Toole & Dunn 2002).

The contribution of drama and literacy was not a focus of my PhD research, but drama as pedagogy was and so was supporting teachers to develop and innovate in their teaching practice. As a reaction to the initiating event of a door opening through the drama literacy program, I, the protagonist in the narrative, responded with the statement of a goal.

A drama literacy and teacher capacity building program (4. Emotional response or statement of goal by the protagonist)

My goal was to be able to apply my research findings to the real-world context of schools. I wanted to support teachers in creating deeper student learning experiences through ongoing, in-situ professional learning. My research and experience could support and guide the development of the drama and literacy program but there was more for me to learn about the needs of literacy learning in schools often with students from EAL (English as an additional language), disadvantaged and culturally diverse backgrounds.

CEO team leader Mark Hopkins and I believed the success of combining drama and literacy lay with classroom teachers empowering themselves to develop and innovate, and could only be supported systemically if we had data and results. I had concluded in my PhD research that innovation and change in schools could only be achieved with the integration of a 'bottom-up' and 'top-down' approach. My research supported Darling-Hammond's (2005) view that:

'Neither a heavy-handed view of top down reform nor a romantic vision of bottom-up change is plausible. Both local intervention and

---

language by analysing the relationships between texts, language, social groups and social practices.

supportive leadership are needed, along with new horizontal efforts that support cross-school consultation and learning' (366).

To implement and sustain pedagogical and curriculum change, Fullan, Hill and Crévola (2006) argue that it is necessary to personalise and precisely meet the student's learning needs and deliver ongoing organisational and collaborative professional learning for teachers. But Groundwater-Smith and Mockler (2009) describe how the recent rise of a compliant culture in education does not encourage and support teachers to have the professional judgment and courage to reflect, question and innovate through 'bottom-up' initiatives. Groundwater-Smith and Mockler (2009) contend that the practices of 'top-down', inflexible auditing and standardising in education, and a lack of systematic support for active, explorative and inventive teacher practice have generated a compliance agenda in schools and the curriculum.

It is with these concerns – about a compliance culture in education, the need to cater to student learning needs in situ and to integrate bottom-up and top-down professional learning approaches to effectively build teacher capacity – that I set out to achieve my goal, to use my research to make a difference. In life as with stories there are complicating factors and obstacles. With the drama literacy program it began by getting school principals and teachers to understand something they hadn't come across before. The program also opened up issues in learning beyond drama and literacy.

Problems and pedagogy in schools (5. Complicating actions)

Innovation is often hard to sell. This was the first problem or complicating action encountered in the fore story narrative. School leaders were unsure what the drama literacy program was. They didn't have an established model of drama literacy learning on which to base their understanding. They also didn't have a model for a teacher capacity-building program that involved theatre artists, classroom teachers and an academic mentor (me) working together with students in situ on an ongoing basis.

The drama literacy program was innovative and novel like any creative idea. Often new ideas are rejected because the crowd does not realise that a proposed idea represents a valid and advanced way of thinking (Sternberg 2003). Upsetting the status quo is perceived as annoying and irrelevant. The status quo in primary schools is that drama learning exists on the fringes and is usually treated as 'relief face to face'. To give the classroom teacher relief time, drama is taught by a casual teacher for a lesson perhaps once a week for half a year (at best) to each class in the school. Connecting drama pedagogy to literacy development and capacity-building in classroom teachers who perceive themselves as 'non-specialists' in drama, and presenting professional learning as an ongoing action learning enterprise and not as a one-off workshop, challenged the status quo.

The compliance agenda and a perceived crowded curriculum meant schools seemed unable to make space for innovation. It could not be assumed that the drama literacy program as a new and creative idea would sell itself. The idea and value of the program needed to be sold. Not in terms of the monetary cost of the program for it was funded by CEO at Parramatta and later through Low SES School Communities National Partnership government funding direct to the schools. Energy had to be spent convincing school leaders to come on board. It was only through the success of the program in one willing school, that momentum began to grow in 'selling' the program to other schools. For the program to be taken up and developed it needs not only top-down support from the CEO as an administrative and policy system, but also willing bottom-up support from schools and teachers.

Another complicating action was caused by the program beginning to develop into something more than drama and literacy. Through observation of the program and professional conversations with participating teachers I realised 'innovation' in the program was more than learning through embodiment and role playing to achieve engagement and empathy in literacy. I realised that in the follow-up literacy tasks finding the 'elements' or the essentials to deeper learning through scaffolding and creative and critical thinking were further supporting and developing teachers in the primary classroom.

Initially the drama lessons were a link to suggested literacy exercises for the classroom teacher to undertake. The accompanying literacy tasks are now a model program in scaffolded and sequenced units in literacy through creative and critical pedagogy for deeper learning. Creative pedagogy can be described as the interrelated elements of creative teaching, teaching for creativity and creative learning (Lin 2011). Critical pedagogy (Freire 2006 [1970]) proposes that education can be socially transforming by actively engaging students to question, critique and challenge.

The classroom teachers use the creative and critical learning tasks to focus on other codes and structures in literacy representation, purpose and audience. These literacy tasks spring from the experiential, performative and narrative processes of the drama literacy lessons. Some of the schools are now exploring drama pedagogy in other curriculum areas such as 'Human society and its environment'. The program also leads the primary classes to create performances for their school community based on the picture books or topics of study.

These complications or developments in the program all resonated with findings I had made in my PhD research. In my research I had recommended that deep and scaffolded, creative and critical learning needed to be developed in film and media arts. I had concluded that effective film learning used experiential and performative processes of learning, and narrative and performative codes of representation for an audience. I now realised what was 'a given' in drama pedagogy was not only relevant to film learning but also relevant to literacy learning and really all learning. What is best in drama pedagogical practice is creative and critical pedagogy that should be applied across the curriculum.

Creative and critical pedagogy however has no relevance if students cannot concentrate on learning. In some of the schools with poor literacy and numeracy skills, characterised by EAL learners, or those from low socio-economic and culturally diverse backgrounds, there is the complicating issue of students being challenged to focus and imagine in their once-a-week drama literacy lesson. Students' staying focused is a problem across many of the learning environments in these particular schools. Drama made the problem more obvious and apparent, and has revealed deeper learning issues.

These socialisation and learning issues may be supported in part through the techniques and processes of drama pedagogy. Effective drama pedagogy can socialise learning through community and agency (Neelands & Nelson 2013); develop skills in critical thinking, listening and empathy (Chan 2013); activate oracy (O'Toole & Stinson 2013) and writing skills (Dunn, Harden & Marino 2013); motivate language learning and use (Stinson & Piazzoli 2013); and help students envision and rehearse alternative modes of action for personal and social change (Cahill 2013). The learning issues in these disadvantaged schools are complex and require a unified, sustained and multi-faceted approach towards teacher and leadership capacity-building, and systemic support.

As with the PhD research backstory, complicating actions are the problems and tension that further our understanding and knowledge. By applying the PhD research to the drama literacy program my understanding of drama, creative and critical pedagogy and deep-focused learning was given an opportunity to develop

Conclusion (6. Outcome)

The drama literacy program has been running for a year and the findings so far have shaped its ongoing development. The program is developed through constant reflection in-action and research with all the participants. It is not a program where one size fits all; it is a program where teachers endeavour to find complex solutions to complex problems. I hope through development, refinement and tangible data and outcomes it will gain funding to become a program that is effective in making a difference for students across a wider range of schools. It does however fly in the face of the compliance and reductionist agenda so prevalent in the education system today. The program is working to create and support literacy and the development of learning through essential scaffolds, critical and creative pedagogy, process and performative drama learning experiences and forging stronger links across the curriculum in deeper learning.

The effectiveness of the program is measured by data collected by participating teachers and responses from the students. The data are observations by the teachers of their students' development and work samples collected. Teachers acknowledge that learning has impacted upon students' engagement with literacy tasks and has opened up a broader understanding and development of multimodal literacy. Students who rarely shine in other classroom literacy exercises are engaged and contributing higher order thinking in discussions in the drama literacy lessons. In schools where there is stronger literacy and focused socialised learning environments, teachers observed in students an increase in collaborative skills, social confidence, creativity and critical thinking.

Average literacy students are more engaged with their writing, and formulate their writing better through the aid of the literacy scaffolds. The experience of deeper learning with one picture book or stimulus over two terms in the drama lessons and literacy tasks is encouraging a deeper engagement with literacy and with learning. The literacy tasks are challenging but students are showing more insight, imagination and skill in their writing. Embodied drama pedagogy contributes to these skills and understandings but just as important are the scaffolds and creative and critical pedagogy applied to the follow-up literacy tasks. Students' talking and listening, and creative and critical thinking is gradually being developed in the once-a-week drama literacy lessons. In socially disadvantaged schools the students are slowly learning how to learn through drama, and learning how to focus on and engage with learning.

What is also integral to the program is the collaborative and sustained capacity-building of teachers. The program is a partnership with teachers and provides other ways to explore literacy learning. In the individual schools a mini 'community of practice' has been created through the relationships and mutual endeavours of teachers, visiting theatre artists, students and me as researcher and mentor. We have an opportunity for professional conversations where we share, reflect upon and develop our professional practice through feedback and research.

The challenges to develop and 'sell' the ideas and value of the program are surmounted when the reaction from teachers, students and school leaders is positive. In one school participating teachers in the program have 'moved out of their comfort zone' and are leading drama literacy in other classes across the school. The drama performances evolving from the program develop and profile arts pedagogy in the school community, curriculum and learning culture. Innovation, evolution and vibrancy in learning is happening in these schools because teachers, school and systemic leaders are willing to 'invest in creativity' (Sternberg 2003).

The 'findings in action' as the outcome is the not the end of the story. The end is the reaction to the outcome, and in essence it is the focus of this chapter and why I wrote it for *State of the art*.

The possibilities of research and drama pedagogy (7. Reactions to outcome)

The premise of this chapter is that research and drama pedagogy has continued to open doors to possibility. The insights gained so far through the drama literacy program and my preceding PhD research lead me to conclude they are ongoing narratives. They are not cyclic like an absurdist play by Beckett, but move forward into the future with cause and effect. They are also not a French farce with opening and closing doors going nowhere.

Doing research can empower drama teachers to develop their practice and make a difference to student and teacher learning. To dwell in the house of possibility is to take the journey of possibility but it takes courage to meet adversity, and challenges, and time for creative and critical thinking. The key to the ongoing research narrative is opportunity and collaboration. The story doesn't exist without the dynamic and passionate teachers, researchers and visionaries who have been there on my journey of possibility.

The possibility inherent in drama pedagogy opens up a critical understanding of learning more generally. Drama pedagogy is multifaceted in its learning approach; it is embodied, enacted and social; it uses creative, critical and reflective thought; it is authentic, rich and collaborative, and combines cognitive thought with our emotions. Drama guides us to an understanding that deep and effective learning combines a creative and critical pedagogy scaffolded for the empowerment of students and teachers alike.

When defining deeper learning, The National Research Council of the National Academies (NRC) (2012) developed three domains that cluster competencies necessary for students in the 21st century: the cognitive, the intrapersonal and the interpersonal. The cognitive domain includes competencies such as critical thinking, information literacy and innovation. The intrapersonal is the ability to be flexible, show initiative, appreciate diversity and reflect on one's own learning. The interpersonal domain contains competencies in communication, collaboration and responsibility. It all sounds like drama pedagogy. Research is showing how cognition is supported by intra and interpersonal skills, and that cognition skills increase positive interpersonal skills (NRC, 2012).

Learning experiences that promote and support the cognitive, the intra- and interpersonal domains are more likely to achieve deeper learning, that is learning that is transferable from one situation and another. These are skills needed for the 21st century. Drama pedagogy has demonstrated to me how the skills and knowledge in the cognitive, intra- and interpersonal domains can be confluent in the classroom.

Drama pedagogy is illustrative of what all learning processes should aim to be: scaffolded and deep, creative and critical, collaborative and affirming. The 'drama literacy program' I am working on may soon lose its nomenclature. In reality, the program is becoming 'creative and critical pedagogy for deeper learning'. This is the power of research and drama pedagogy in the ongoing narrative of students and teachers learning. A school principal has asked me what the drama literacy program can do about numeracy. Another door opens . . .

Works cited

Anderson M, Hughes J & Manuel J (Eds) (2008). *Drama and English teaching: imagination, action and engagement.* South Melbourne: Oxford University Press.

Anderson M & Jefferson M (2009). *Teaching the screen: film education for generation next.* Sydney: Allen and Unwin.

Aubusson P, Ewing R & Hoban G (2009). *Action learning in schools: reframing teachers' professional learning and development.* London, New York: Routledge.

Belliveau G & Prendergast M (2013). Drama and literature: masks and love potions. In M Anderson & J Dunn (Eds). *How drama activates learning: contemporary research and practice* (pp277–90). London: Bloomsbury.

Branigan E (1992). *Narrative comprehension and film.* London: Routledge.

Brown R (2005). Learning communities and the nature of teacher participation in a learning community. *Literacy learning: the middle years,* 13(2): 8–15.

Bruner J (1987). Life as narrative. *Social Research,* 54(1): 11–32.

Cahill H (2013). Drama for health and human relationships education: aligning purpose and design. In M Anderson & J Dunn (Eds). *How drama activates learning: contemporary research and practice* (pp178–92). London: Bloomsbury.

Chan Y (2013). Drama and global citizenship education: planting seeds of social conscience and change. In M Anderson & J Dunn (Eds). *How drama activates learning: contemporary research and practice* (pp78–93). London: Bloomsbury.

Chase S E (2008). Narrative inquiry: multiple approaches, voices. In NK Denzin & YS Lincoln (Eds). *Collecting and interpreting qualitative materials* (pp57–94). Thousand Oaks: SAGE Publications.

Clandinin DJ & Connelly FM (1994). Personal experience methods. In NK Denzin & YS Lincoln (Eds). *Handbook of qualitative research* (pp413–27). Thousand Oaks: SAGE Publications.

Corbin J & Strauss A (2008). *Basics of qualitative research: techniques and procedures for developing grounded theory*. Thousand Oaks: SAGE Publications.

Darling-Hammond L (2005). Policy and change: getting beyond bureaucracy. In A Hargreaves (Ed). *Extending educational change* (pp362–87). Dordrecht: Springer.

Dewey J (1958). *Experience and nature*. New York: Dover.

Dunn J, Harden A & Marino S (2013). Drama and writing: overcoming the hurdle of the blank page. In M Anderson & J Dunn (Eds). *How drama activates learning: contemporary research and practice* (pp245–59). London: Bloomsbury.

Ewing R (2009). Creating imaginative, practical possibilities in K–6 English classrooms. In J Manuel, P Brock, D Carter & W Sawyer (Eds). *Imagination, innovation, creativity: re-envisioning English in education* (pp171–82), Putney: Phoenix Education

Ewing R (2010). *Curriculum and assessment: a narrative approach*. South Melbourne: Oxford University Press.

Ewing R, Miller C, & Saxton J (2008). Drama and contemporary picture books in the middle years. In M Anderson, J Hughes & J Manuel. (Eds). *Drama and English teaching: imagination, action and engagement* (pp121–35). South Melbourne: Oxford University Press.

Ewing R & Simons J (2004). *Beyond the script take 2: drama for the classroom*. Sydney: Primary English Teaching Association.

Freire P (2006 [1970]). *Pedagogy of the oppressed*. MB Ramos, Trans. New York, London: Continuum.

Freebody P (2003). *Qualitative research in education: interaction and practice*. London: SAGE Publications.

Fullan M, Hill P & Crévola C (2006). *Breakthrough*. Thousand Oaks: Corwin Press.

Gibson R & Ewing R (2011). *Transforming the curriculum through the arts*. Sydney: Palgrave.

Greenwood D J & Levin M (2008). Reform of the social sciences, and of universities through action research. In NK Denzin & YS Lincoln (Eds). *The landscape of qualitative research* (pp57–86). Thousand Oaks: SAGE Publications.

Groundwater-Smith S & Mockler N (2009). *Teacher professional learning in an age of compliance*. Dordrecht: Springer.

Hargreaves A (2003). *Teaching in the knowledge society: education in the age of insecurity*. New York: Teachers College Press.

Hofer M & Owings-Swan K (2005). Digital moviemaking – the harmonization of technology, pedagogy and content. *International Journal of Technology in Teaching and Learning*, 1(2): 102–10.

Hughes J (1991). *Drama in education: the state of the art, an Australian perspective*. Rozelle, NSW: Educational Drama Association.

Jefferson M (2011). Film learning as aesthetic experience: dwelling in the house of possibility. PhD thesis, University of Sydney, Sydney.

Kincheloe JL & McLaren P (2005). Rethinking critical theory and qualitative research. In NK Denzin & YS Lincoln (Eds). *The Sage handbook of qualitative research* (pp303–42). Thousand Oaks: SAGE Publications.

Lave J & Wenger E (1991). *Situated learning: legitimate peripheral participation*. Cambridge, MA: Cambridge University Press.

Lin Y (2011). Fostering creativity through education – a conceptual framework of creative pedagogy. *Creative Education*, 2(3): 149–55.

Miller C & Saxton J (2004). *Into the story: language in action through drama*. Portsmouth, NH: Heinemann.

Moran S & John-Steiner V (2003). Creativity in the making: Vygotsky's contemporary contribution to the dialectic of development and creativity. In RK Sawyer, V John-Steiner, S Moran, RJ Sternberg, DH Feldman, J Nakamura & M Csikszentmihalyi (Eds), *Creativity and development* (pp61–90). New York: Oxford University Press.

National Research Council of the National Academies (2012). *Education for life and work: developing transferable knowledge and skills in the 21st century*. Washington, DC: National Academies Press. [Online] www.nap.edu/catalog.php?record_id=13398 [Accessed 16 August 2013]

Neelands J (1992). *Learning through imagined experience: teaching English in the national curriculum*. London: Hodder and Stoughton Educational.

Neelands J & Nelson B (2013). Drama, community and achievement: together I'm someone. In M Anderson & J Dunn (Eds). *How drama activates learning: contemporary research and practice* (pp15–29). London: Bloomsbury.

NRC see National Research Council of the National Academies.

O'Mara J (2008). Reading and writing ourselves into the twenty-first century. In M Anderson, J Hughes and J Manuel (Eds). *Drama and English teaching: imagination, action and engagement*. South Melbourne Oxford University Press.

O'Toole J & Dunn J (2002). *Pretending to learn: helping children learn through drama*. Frenchs Forest: Pearson Education.

O'Toole J & Stinson M (2013). Drama, speaking and listening: the treasure of oracy. In M Anderson & J Dunn (Eds). *How drama activates learning: contemporary research and practice* (pp159–77). London: Bloomsbury.

O'Toole J & Stinson M (2009). Curriculum: the house that Jack built. In J O'Toole, M Stinson & T Moore, (Eds). *Drama and curriculum: a giant at the door* (pp29–45). Dordrecht: Springer.

Patton MQ (2002). *Qualitative research and evaluation methods*. Thousand Oaks: SAGE Publications.

Pedler M (1996). Introduction. In M Pedler (Ed). *Action learning in practice* (pxxix–xxxii). Hampshire Gower Publishing.

Pinar WF, Reynolds WM, Slattery P & Taubman PM (1995). *Understanding curriculum: an introduction to the study of historical and contemporary curriculum discourses*. New York: Peter Lang.

Revans RW (1980). *Action learning: new techniques for management*. London: Blond and Briggs.

Sartre JP (1981). *The family idiot: Gustave Flaubert, 1821–1857* (Vol. 1). C. Cosman, Trans. Chicago: University of Chicago Press.

Saxton J & Miller C (2009). Drama: bridging the conversations between our inner selves and the outside world. *English in Australia*, 44(2): 35–42.

Saxton J & Miller C (2013). Drama, creating and imagining: rendering the world newly strange. In M Anderson & J Dunn (Eds). *How drama activates learning: contemporary research and practice* (pp111–24). London: Bloomsbury.

Stake RE (1978). The case study method in a social inquiry. *Educational Researcher*, 7(2): 5–8.

Stake RE (2008). Qualitative case studies. In NK Denzin & YS Lincoln (Eds). *Strategies of qualitative inquiry* (pp119–49). Thousand Oaks: SAGE Publications.

Sternberg RJ (2003). *Wisdom, intelligence, and creativity synthesized*. New York: Cambridge University Press

Stinson M & Piazzoli E (2013). Drama for additional language learning: dramatic contexts and pedagogical possibilities. In M Anderson & J Dunn (Eds). *How drama activates learning: contemporary research and practice* (pp208–25). London: Bloomsbury.

2
School drama: towards state of the art in drama professional learning?

Robyn Ewing, Robyn Gibson, Victoria Campbell, John Saunders and Helen Hristofski

The role of quality arts experiences in nurturing who we are as people alongside their ability to enhance creative learning across the curriculum is well documented and has enjoyed a renaissance over the last decade (eg, President's Committee on the Humanities and Social Sciences 2011; Caldwell & Vaughan 2012; Gibson & Ewing 2011; Ewing 2010; Catterall 2009; Bamford 2006: Bryce et al. 2004; Deasy 2002; Fiske 1999). An arts-rich curriculum can be a powerful agent in developing an inclusive classroom learning community where teachers and students think critically and express their understanding while creatively respecting a multiplicity of perspectives (Burnaford, et al. 2001).

In particular, the importance of seeing educational or process drama as critical, quality pedagogy (Ewing 2012, 2010, 2006; McCarthy et al. 2006; O'Toole & Dunn 2002; O'Neill 1995) as well as understanding drama as a specific art form has also been well researched. As O'Connor (2008, 29) asserts:

Ewing R, Gibson R, Campbell V, Saunders J & Hristofski H (2015). School drama: towards the state of the art in drama professional learning? In M Anderson & C Roche (Eds). *The state of the art: teaching drama in the 21st century*, (25–48). Sydney: Sydney University Press.

we must recognise the absolute centrality of drama in giving a sense of what it is to be other than ourselves in a world where otherness and difference is often something to be feared and punished.

There is also a wealth of evidence that demonstrates the powerful role that drama strategies can play in improving students' English language and literacy outcomes (eg Dunn & Stinson 2011; Ewing 2010, 2006; Ewing & Simons 2004; Miller & Saxton 2004; Baldwin & Fleming 2003). Recent neuroscientific evidence further provides an underpinning for many of the understandings about learning that drama and other arts educators have known from many years of professional practice (eg Baldwin 2012; Ewing 2010).

Despite this, a significant number of generalist primary teachers report that they lack the expertise and/or the confidence to use drama for any substantive activity within their classrooms. In numerous instances, drama, when implemented at all, is employed as a fun 'fill-in' activity or as a warm-up game before the 'real' work begins. As a result, it is often undervalued and underused, both as a discipline in its own right and as pedagogy across the curriculum (Ewing et al. 2011, 33). While the incoming Australian arts curriculum mandates two hours of arts each week in all F–10[1] Australian classrooms, the increasing regulatory, high-stakes national testing regime has already resulted in a narrowing of the curriculum for primary students. Such technical approaches to assessment place pressure on teachers to teach to tests and to feel they must concentrate on transmissive and traditional approaches to the teaching of literacy and numeracy. As a result, drama remains at risk of remaining on the fringe of the primary curriculum.

Similarly, children's literature has not been as prominent a feature of every primary classroom in recent years. Research suggests (eg Cremin, et al. 2008) that many primary teachers lack the confidence to choose quality literary texts for close study in their classroom. For example, Cremin et al. reveal that the 1200 primary professionals in their 2008 study leaned on a narrow repertoire of authors, poets and picture book artists. In defining quality texts Libby Gleeson (2012, 6) writes that:

---

1 The incoming Australian curriculum uses the term 'Foundation' to denote the first year of school.

A quality text must have integrity. It must have characters that are fully realised. It must have language that fully expresses what the writer wants to say. The story must satisfy the reader but also make demands of the reader. The very best stories have something to say that goes beyond a surface meaning to something deeper, a symbolic meaning that speaks of the human condition.

The declining number of school librarians in many Australian states due to funding cuts has exacerbated this trend. Often unrecognised as an art form and omitted from the incoming *Australian curriculum: the arts*, literature is the art form that most Australians recognise and engage with (Australia Council, 2010).

Enabling teachers to bring two art forms, drama and quality children's literature together, to equip children with sophisticated literacy skills is the core of the School Drama[2] program, described in more detail in the next section.

The School Drama (SD) program

Developed largely as a response to this context and building on Ewing's classroom work in drama, literature and literacy with primary teachers over more than 25 years, this chapter reports on the findings of five years of SD, a program developed in 2009 through a partnership between the Sydney Theatre Company (STC)[3] and the Faculty of Education and Social Work (ESW), University of Sydney.[4] SD focuses specifically on developing primary teachers' professional knowledge of and expertise in the use of process drama with children's literature to enhance their students' English and literacy outcomes. The program is based on an authentic understanding of partnership and a co-mentoring approach to teacher professional learning (Aubusson et al. 2009; Le Cornu 2005) and has been largely funded by STC's philanthropic

---

2 http://www.sydneytheatre.com.au/community/education/teacher-professional-learning/school-drama.aspx
3 Sydney Theatre Company has been a major force in Australian theatre since it was founded in the 1970s. The current Artistic Director is Andrew Upton.
4 An earlier discussion of SDS can be found in Ewing et al. (2011).

foundation and, in 2013–14, Origin Energy. The section below briefly addresses these principles before describing the SD process and discussing its outcomes to date. The final section considers the implications of the program and future directions.

Partnership

The SD program is dependent on a partnership not just between STC and the ESW but between each educator and teaching artist working towards student academic achievement in a particular classroom: in this instance, improvement in identified English and literacy outcomes. Both levels of partnership need to be authentic (Auerbach 2012, 5) and therefore must ensure a respectful alliance between educators and artists, value the building of a relationship, engage in healthy dialogue across differences, and ensure power is shared. Teachers and artists working in collaborative ventures need to develop a respect and appreciation of each others' 'skills set' (Upitis 2005) if such a partnership is to succeed. This partnership is thus a significant departure from many artists-in-residence programs.

The partnership between STC and the ESW:

- support participant teachers to engage with drama and quality literature within their classrooms
- provide quality professional learning experiences through STC performers/artists modelling the use of drama strategies and techniques as pedagogical tools, particularly in English and literacy learning
- improve students' learning outcomes in English and literacy
- foster teachers' enthusiasm and confidence in being associated with a working theatre which would thereby enhance the creative processes of their students and create a sustainable model for artists and teachers to work together in schools to enhance curriculum outcomes rather than the traditional 'artist-in-residence' approach.

Professional learning

SD seeks to develop primary teachers' professional knowledge of and expertise in the use of process drama. Actors, or teaching artists, work in a co-mentoring relationship alongside classroom teachers once a week for up to seven weeks in either term two, three or four of the school year. There is a strong emphasis on teacher ownership and professional responsibility in the co-mentoring model and this professional learning model is a defining feature of SD. Teaching artists model the use of drama strategies with quality literary texts to address a specific literacy or English outcome that has been identified by the class teacher. The intention of the program is that the teachers will then continue to use their new-found expertise in drama with quality texts with their own students and hopefully with other classes at their school. While anecdotal evidence teachers affirm that it is their intention to continue to use the drama strategies in this way, the long-term sustainability of the program is critical and the 2013–14 meta-analysis and ongoing case studies seek to confirm that this is the case. Teachers often work with a teaching artist for two successive years to consolidate and further develop their understandings and expertise. The following quotes are representative of teacher interview feedback at the conclusion of their work with the teaching artist:

> I thought it was exciting to work with someone with extensive theatrical background, who is working in the industry, they have more insight than a classroom teacher . . . yes I did develop some skills . . .

> For me it was like mentoring in drama teaching . . . [the teaching artist] broke it down in a way that made me realise I could do it. It was empowering. It was fantastic. I have been using some of those activities . . . I would love to have more.

Co-mentoring

As mentioned earlier, the professional learning model is conceptualised as a co-mentoring approach. Instead of using the traditional conception of the mentor as the expert, reconceptualising the mentoring process as one of co-learning positions the participants in a non-hierarchical or reciprocal relationship (Le Cornu 2005; Bona et al. 1995, 119). The teachers learn about the use of drama in enhancing literacy and English while the teaching artists learn about adapting their professional theatre skills to a particular literacy focus in classroom contexts. One of the teaching artists articulates this clearly comparing his experience working with two teachers:

> It's really that building of the relationship between the teacher and the teaching artist that's so crucial. I realise now how important that is because I've had the experience where it didn't happen and now I know it's crucial for the program and that it works very well. (Roger)

The participants

The program's effectiveness is demonstrated by its popularity in Sydney classrooms. Table 2.1 summarises the growth of SD since 2009.

The SD process

All teachers undertake an initial full day workshop in which they engage in drama strategies with contemporary picture books. In many instances the principals of the participating schools attend the first session of this workshop and subsequently have invited Ewing and Saunders to present a workshop for their whole school staff. The teacher workshop ensures that the teachers have experienced the strategies for themselves and removes the fear that drama can only be taught by skilled, specialist professionals. Many come to this initial workshop with 'baggage' and insecurities from their own past experiences at school. Teachers and teaching artists then meet to plan their program and the teachers identify the English or literacy focus. Table 2.2 provides an overview of the 2011 outcomes and literary texts by class in each classroom.

Quality literary texts are usually selected at this initial planning session. Often the teaching artist will suggest an appropriate text based on their experience in earlier years. The teaching artist then plans seven

Table 2.1 SD statistics

Year	Teachers (ranging from early career to 30+ years exp)	Teaching artists	Students in primary classrooms (K–6)	Schools
2009	11	2	c.250	5 disadvantaged inner city
2010	26	4	600+*	15, diverse range, across all school sectors
2011	35	7	845+	17, diverse range, across all school sectors
2012	39	5	960 +	23, diverse range across all sectors and including 3 in Broken Hill
2013	58	12	1450 +	Included 3 schools in Broken Hill and Interstate pilot in Adelaide
2014	92	15	2760 +	Over 40 schools, 3 in Blue Mountains and interstate pilot continued in Adelaide

* One intensive English class (13–18 year olds) was also involved in addition to this estimate of primary students.

90–120 minute sessions usually implemented over seven weeks. Ewing provides support and advice to the actors in terms of potential resources and strategies. Over time STC has built a resource file of units of work developed and it is anticipated that these will be available online and in published book form in 2015. Ongoing access to this resource has been identified by the teachers in each year of the evaluations as an important way they will be able to source other unit plans after the teaching artist has moved to other classrooms.

This planning is shared with the teacher prior to the commencement of the sessions and the classroom teacher designs an appropriate benchmarking task that case study students undertake prior to and after the program. The teaching artist then models the use of various drama strategies with the texts each week and often follow-up tasks are completed before their next visit. Gradually the classroom teacher develops confidence to use drama strategies either between visits from the

Table 2.2 2011 SD program

	Group*	Aims	Text
1	Yr2 (19)	Talking and listening – deeper engagement with text	*The great expedition* by Peter Carnavas
2	Yr3 (22)	Descriptive writing – greater understanding of narratives	*Pinquo* by Colin Thiele
3	Yr2 (25)	Reading/writing – understanding narrative structure	*Rose meets Mr Wintergarten* by Bob Graham
4	Yr3/4 (25)	Writing – developing understanding of inference in texts	*The werewolf knight* by Jenny Wagner
5	Yr4 (27)	Reading/writing – developing deeper level of comprehension (critical thinking)	*The lost thing* by Shaun Tan
6	Yr3 (27)	Reading/writing – deeper level of comprehension	*The rabbits* by John Marsden & Shaun Tan
7	Yr1 (30)	Talking/listening /writing – narrative structure	*Who's afraid of the big bad book* by Lauren Child
8	Yrs 3/4 (30)	Talking/listening – personal connections with text	*The miraculous journey of Edward Tulane* by Kate Di Camillo
9	Yr3/4 (25)	Reading/writing – deeper level of comprehension	*My place* by Nadia Wheatley & Donna Rawlins
10	Yr2 (24)	Descriptive writing – expression & fluency	*Rain dance* by Cathy Applegate & Dee Huxley
11	Yr3/4 (30)	Reading/writing – deeper level of comprehension	*The lost thing* by Shaun Tan
12	K (10)	Reading – comprehension (Who? Where? When? What happened? How & why?)	*The great paper caper* by Oliver Jeffers

2 School drama

	Group*	Aims	Text
13	K (10)	Reading – comprehension (Who? Where? When? What happened? How & why?)	*The great paper caper* by Oliver Jeffers
14	Yr6 (30)	Speaking & listening – confidence in oral communication	*Macbeth & son* by Jackie French
15	Yr1/2 (24)	Reading & writing – developing critical thinking skills	*The very best of friends* by Margaret Wild & Julie Vivas
16	K (21)	Speaking & listening – confidence in oral communication	*Marshall Armstrong is new to our school* by David Mackintosh
17	Yr3 (30)	Reading & writing – improving narrative writing	*The lost thing* by Shaun Tan
18	Yr6 (22)	Reading & writing – narrative & deeper level of comprehension	*My place* by Nadia Wheatley & Donna Rawlins
19	Yr3 (21)	Reading & writing – information reports	*Iron man* by Ted Hughes
20	Yrs3/4 (28)	Reading & writing – increased vocab & adjectives for descriptive writing	*The lost thing* by Shaun Tan
21	Yr5/6 (29)	Reading & writing – detail in narrative writing	*The lion, the witch & the wardrobe* by C. S. Lewis
22	K/1 (19)	Talking & listening – understanding of whole story structure	*Where the wild things are* by Maurice Sendak
23	Yrs3–6 (22)	Speaking & listening – confidence in oral communication ie expressive voice, body & gesture	*Bambert's book of missing stories* by Reinhardt Jung
24	Yr4 (29)	Reading & writing – develop understanding of narrative structure	*The lost thing* by Shaun Tan

The state of the art

	Group*	Aims	Text
25	Yr4 (28)	Writing talking & listening – deeper understanding of character & place	*The miraculous journey of Edward Tulane* by Kate DiCamillo
26	Yr6 (25)	Descriptive language – character, location & events	*The burnt stick* by Anthony Hill
27	Yr6 (25)	Descriptive language – character, location & events	*The burnt stick* by Anthony Hill
28	Yr6 (25)	Descriptive language – character, location & events	*The burnt stick* by Anthony Hill
29	K (23)	Speaking & listening – oral communication ie making personal connections with text	*Marshall Armstrong is new to our school* by David Mackintosh; *Lost and found* by Oliver Jeffers
30	Yr3/4 (25)	Reading & writing – increased vocabulary ie written & oral	*Angry Mangry* by Barton Williams; *Phileas's fortune: a story about self-expression* by Agnes de Lestrade & Valeria Docompo
31	Yr4/5 (24)	Descriptive writing – developing an understanding & expression of character	*The magic paintbrush* by Robin Muller
32	Yr2/3 (23)	Reading & writing – developing a deeper level of comprehension & understanding of narrative structure	*Diary of a wimpy kid* by Jeff Kinney
33	Yr3/4 (25)	Reading & writing – comprehension of narrative structure	*The lion, the witch & the wardrobe* by C. S. Lewis
34	K (18)	Talking & listening – comprehension of story, time & place	*Mr Gumpy's outing* by John Burningham; *There's a sea in my bedroom* by Jane Tanner

Group*	Aims	Text
35 Yr2 (24)	Reading & writing – deeper level of comprehension	*Going home* by Eve Bunting

Source: Gibson 2012. *Group includes year and number of students.

teaching artist or with other classes. In addition many teachers begin to see the potential for using drama in other curriculum areas.

Expectations

The teachers involved in SD either express an interest in being part of SD or are selected by their principal. In their pre-program questionnaire the majority of the teachers state that they need to develop their skills to teach drama in the classroom. Most also express some excitement about developing an understanding of the links between drama and literacy learning. While some have had experience teaching drama, either in their classroom or in their pre-service teacher education program, they often feel they need to develop more skills to teach it effectively. Typical comments in their pre-program interviews include:

> I would like to be more familiar and more confident – to step in every day and teach drama from the top of my head. Because the things that might hold you back as a teacher is preparedness, so I would like to be familiar and more comfortable . . . to have the skills at my finger tips.

> I touch on it, we have done some Readers' Theatre, but I confess, I only do the odd drama game on the occasional afternoon, it is not consistent.

> I would like to have the skills to link literacy and drama and explore picture books without having to follow the lessons of others to be able to create my own lesson.

> I have been teaching for long time and I am a bit stale on some ideas, I believe in the creative arts, but drama is not one of my strong points.

The development of new drama skills is also encouraged by some of the principals who clearly understand the important link between drama and literacy learning. One principal who understands the power of drama to engage students, commented:

> I would like to think of it as an opportunity to inspire the staff. As a result I hope that there is an increased opportunity for us all to discuss what it is that really engages kids. For the kids I hope there is an opportunity for them to reflect on this experience and continue to develop ownership of this process, so that it is something we can continue to build on within the school community...

Findings

The participant teachers respond to a series of interview questions before and after the SD program either by telephone or email. In addition, in 2011 nine teachers were selected for face-to-face in-depth interviews conducted by a research assistant. Several in-depth school case studies have been undertaken. The actors have also been interviewed. In some classes, students have also provided responses in focus groups.

As previously stated, SD focuses on two interrelated outcomes:

- the role of a partnership between artists and educators in order to foster professional learning in the use of drama with literature to enhance academic achievement
- the role of process drama and literary texts in improving student English and literacy learning.

The role of a partnership to foster professional learning

In the vast majority of instances, the in-class professional learning that occurred during the SD developed the teachers' confidence to embed drama strategies in English and literacy programming using authentic literacy texts. Overwhelmingly, and consistently to date (Campbell et al. 2010) the participant teachers have reported a range of positive outcomes both in terms of their students' English and literacy development and their own professional learning. The teaching artists and students have also expressed their belief that SD has been beneficial. Benchmarking student achievement before and after the class program has improved, although some teachers did not engage optimally in this analysis phase and this process has been revised.

The following teacher comments are indicative of the teacher responses to SD:

> The program was invaluable. I think that I grew so much as a person, as a teacher, the children grew along with me, and I think I've inspired the other teachers in the school. I just think that it's a fantastic program and I'd love for it to be continued ... Even my supervisor said, 'I'll do whatever I can, I'll take your class for you' ... They are just so passionate about the program that we like to share and give up our time because you guys are doing some great things.

> Personally, it was a very valuable experience that I have shared with my students. In our very busy school lives, there isn't always a lot of time to have fun, laugh and really let go with the children. SD provided this for us, thus strengthening the teacher/student bond and rapport.

> It has been a wonderful enriching experience. It was the highlight of my week ... Predominantly, I learned about the opportunities created by allowing students permission to imagine outside the topic of conversation ... the drama program has allowed me to see the students and their personalities more clearly and share my ideas and personality with them. In this way, I now know know them better and connect with them more meaningfully.

The most successful outcomes were observed when teachers were able to demonstrate the drama strategies to other classes at the school or trial the activities in between the actor's visits (Ewing et al. 2011).

The state of the art

> [The actor] would come on a Tuesday and she would teach my class and I would watch her and I would take notes. I pretty much scripted everything she did. Then on Thursday, the teacher next door ... would teach my class for science and I would take her class. It was really interesting because I got totally different results. Great results. In other words, I was doing side-by-side lessons but I was doing it with another class.

> As a teacher, the importance of using drama in the classroom has given my literacy program greater depth whilst still allowing drama to retain its integrity. Sharing with the staff through a professional development session, I have inspired my colleagues to use drama with literacy to raise student outcomes.

> SD has provided excellent professional development for me. It was very beneficial to see various techniques demonstrated by [the actor] first, and then for me to implement them with my class later in the day/week with the programmed follow-up activities. It gave me the chance to reinforce the concepts and skills and learn with the children.

Many of the SD teachers were able to articulate specific drama skills that they were now confident to use in their classrooms. Initially hesitant to attempt drama activities, one teacher reported:

> working with [the actor] over seven weeks has made me aware of a wide range of techniques and strategies that can enable me to enhance my teaching of all modes of literacy through the use of drama-based experiences. Additionally, I learnt an exciting and stimulating range of warm-up activities, improvisational games and focusing activites which I have continued to use in my class on a regular basis. This was a highly valuable and immediately useful professional development experience.

Another commented that:

> The sense of having a set of skills that are genuinely useful outside a rehearsal room is wonderful and it gives me great pleasure to be

doing something that is so worthwhile. The creative stimulus of this job is deeply rewarding and the sense of positive purpose is great for me… Personally and professionally, this is a very positive experience.

The role of drama and literary texts in student literacy improvement

Most teachers were also enthusiastic about improvements in their students' literacy development.

One Year 2 teacher who was focusing on the development of verbal language skills wrote:

> The drama program has allowed the students to experience literacy outcomes more deeply than was planned for in my English program. The students clearly achieved the proposed indicators for the talking and listening, reading and writing outcomes. They were able to share points of view, respond to texts with unique opinions and alter their voice, intonation, facial expression and gesture, often independently.

Likewise one of the teachers reported on the improvements she observed in her Year 6 class as a result of the program:

> Their responses both oral and written are generally more considered, thoughtful, insightful. They take time to think yet are able to more readily 'think on their feet'. They are able to analyse character's feelings and consequently in their work, more attention is paid to character motivation and voice.

Other benefits for students

Additional benefits for the students, in addition to improvements in literacy learning through drama, were also noted by the teachers. Many comments referred to improved confidence and/or social skills especially related to those students who were perceived as shy, disengaged or marginalised by ability with language and/or other disabilities. For example:

My students have had an opportunity to develop skills outside their previous experience and comfort zones ... With the shy students, or students with special needs, an opportunity for success in front of peers, when there are not many such opportunities academically, raise self-esteem and assist their attitude to other new endeavours.

My students really enjoyed the experience. Every Thursday they would ask 'Is [the actor] coming today?' It was rewarding to see the creativity of some of the children who previously were very shy and didn't join in group activities, become involved and have lots of fun. Confidence was also noted in my students: many students were eager to have a go and join in the activities.

Several teachers noted that Indigenous students had particularly engaged with the drama and storytelling that are at the heart of the SD program.

The students' responses

Although it has not always been appropriate or possible to conduct focus groups with students, many students have expressed their thoughts about SD either in conversations with their teachers, with the teaching artists or in learning journals or through correspondence. Robertson's (2010) case study of one class did enable in-depth focus groups with the participant students. In their discussion they underlined how motivating the drama had been ('deadly') and suggested it should be part of their education each year.

Below are a number of comments from boys in Year 6 class in the 2011 program:

I thought the drama lessons were awesome. They have improved my descriptive writing skills and made my story writing easier to read and more exciting. I really recommend having [the actor] go to other schools and teach other kids what she has taught me.

Drama has helped me with my self-confidence to express my emotions and write them down in words. I learned that there are more layers to our feelings ... I enjoy school now because drama has helped me understand things and why people act in certain ways.

The actors/teaching artists

A study by Barkl (2005, 2) investigating the role of the artist in the Musica Viva program recognised that artists in educational partnerships need to develop other skills beyond their professional artistic skills, if meaningful collaboration between the 'arts sector, the education sector, government and community' are to be reached. The artist, in many instances, needs to develop a pedagogical practice; they need to be able to teach, along with the ability to perform in their chosen field of expertise. It is interesting to note that three of the teaching artists have also sought to undertake teacher education since being involved in the program. One actor in SD discussed this after the first year of the program:

> I have really enjoyed having the world of teaching opened up for me. This style of education I think really works – using drama to teach in something like English has a lot of merit ... However there was a big assumption that this is what actors do, and I had never done any of these things before – it is a fallacy to say we are translating rehearsal techniques into the drama room, it is very different to how you work in rehearsal ... Developing my confidence [with these new skills], I feel useful and that I am doing something worthwhile ... On the whole I have found it stimulating, engaging and satisfying. It's something I would like to continue doing.

These comments led to the introduction of a more intensive workshop program for the teaching artists from 2010 before the teacher workshop. A second meeting is now usually planned for the artists following their first meetings with participant teachers. In 2011 one of the actors commented:

> The sense of having a set of skills that are genuinely useful outside a rehearsal room is wonderful and it gives me great pleasure to be doing something that is so worthwhile. The creative stimulus of this job

> is deeply rewarding and the sense of positive purpose is great for me ... Personally and professionally, this is a very positive experience.

The artists are also now involved in debriefing sessions at the conclusion of each term and again at the end of each year. It is evident that the teachers and artists develop mutual respect for each other and it highlights the importance of the co-mentoring feature of the program. This is a crucial indicator for success in arts education partnerships more generally as well as for the SD process.

Issues: the timeframe

A number of teachers have commented that a longer timeframe would be desirable, especially when attempting to evaluate student literacy learning. Another noted the conflation of SD with other classroom teaching and learning experiences. For example:

> We had a writing focus and I don't feel the program was intensive enough to say that it has contributed to meeting objectives.

> It is difficult to separate other classroom instruction and the drama program in terms of contributions to meeting these objectives.

A majority of the participant teachers believed that deep and lasting learning needs to happen over a sustained period of time. Comments below are reflective of this concern.

> It did improve the students' writing to some extent, but I think it needs to be a longer intervention ...

> The time frame is not long enough: the students are really ripe and it's over.

One teacher wanted her kindergarten students to develop better use of descriptive words in their writing. However while she did see moderate development in this area, she also saw evidence of greater improvement in her students' oral speaking skills with increased ability to tell stories with more confidence, greater expression and better choice of descriptive words. She felt that a 10-week program would have achieved greater results. It is for this reason that the program is now seven-weeks long rather than six although it may have to be condensed for rural and remote contexts for logistic and financial reasons. Funding is the only barrier to a longer program.

Benchmarking

Effective analysis of benchmarking remains an issue, and is raised in each evaluation (Campbell et al. 2010; Gibson 2011, 2012, 2013). Over the pilot years many more teachers have collected detailed and more focused evidence around the identified literacy outcome before and after the intervention, and provided some analysis often as a rubric of the results. Those who did invest time and effort in this important feature of the program have been able to provide clear examples of literacy improvement via student work samples. For example, one year 2 teacher demonstrated that SD has 'contributed greatly to the students' engagement with the text and in developing verbal expression, confidence performing in front of a familiar audience and empathising with the characters in the story'. Her benchmarking consisted of a pre- and post-writing tasks where students were required to describe an imaginary creature, a setting and their interaction with it. It is clear, however, that some teachers need more support in analysis of the data they collect. In 2014 John Saunders and Robyn Ewing developed suggested benchmarking frameworks for oracy, inferential comprehension, descriptive and narrative writing to help teachers with this analysis.

Implications for professional learning in arts and education

One of the most important aspects of the SD program is the professional learning model that underpins the relationship between the teacher and the teaching artist. SD aims to be more than an artist-in-residence program. There is no doubt that the relationship between the artist and the teacher is critical in ensuring that joint planning and careful sequencing is appropriate for the particular group of children involved.

The co-mentoring model acknowledges the artist's expertise and skill in drama but at the same time values the teacher's understanding of his or her students as well as the literacy focus most needed. Teacher and teaching artist work together to select the most appropriate literary texts and to implement the program. Over time the teacher assumes more responsibility for implementation. Similar programs have been developed in other states (see for example the KITE Yonder program developed by Queensland Performing Arts Centre and Education Queensland) and in other art forms (see for example the Australian Ballet's 'Out there: the Australian Ballet in schools'). This kind of teacher professional learning model could and should be more widely used.

In summary, over the last five years, the SD professional learning model has been most successful when:

- a strong relationship between teacher and teaching artist develops
- participating teachers actively model the drama strategies with their own class or with other classes between visits from the teaching artist and hence gain confidence in using them
- careful benchmarking of the identified literacy or English outcome prior to and after the intervention is appropriate and an accompanying detailed analysis is undertaken
- systematic planning occurs in the term prior to the school drama intervention
- there is strong support for the program from the principal/school executive
- teachers work with the same actor over at least two cycles of the program.

The most important next step is to investigate how sustainable SD is once the teaching artists have completed their time in a particular school. Ongoing funding will be needed to research whether this approach to professional learning is valuable long term and whether teachers begin to use drama strategies in other Key Learning Areas as they gain in confidence and expertise.

During 2014 and 2015 the sustainability of School Drama has been investigated with schools that have been participating in the program for more than three years. In addition the Sydney Theatre Company website has included resources and unit plans so that teachers can access units after the conclusion of their work with a teaching artist.

Future steps

In 2012 and 2013 SD was successfully trialled in three schools in a regional and remote context (Gibson 2012). The program was in essence the same. Teachers in each school were able to participate in a professional program although these were held over two sessions after school. Those participating teachers each worked with a teaching artist over seven sessions but these were concentrated over a month rather than seven weeks. More refinement of the program will be needed for remote and regional contexts.

In addition, funding from Origin enabled the program to be piloted successfully in South Australia in 2013–14 and it is hoped that the program will go national in subsequent years. The model will utilise the same partnership model: a state theatre and a state university working together. It is hoped that in time the efficacy of this professional learning model will attract funding from the education systems in each state.

Conclusion

To conclude, the SD program is an innovative example of offering teachers professional learning through co-mentoring with an experienced actor. The findings thus far have been extremely positive with teachers and teaching artists articulating the benefits for their learning as well as evidence of improved student learning in the designated area despite the seven-week timeframe.

The long-term sustainability of the program is currently being investigated. It is clear that the co-mentoring professional learning model has implications beyond the arts and education.

It is of concern, however, that the ongoing potential of such an effective professional learning model is dependent on continued funding by philanthropists and foundations rather than education systems.

The words of one participating teacher from the 2011 SD program provides a valuable final comment:

> It is interesting for me to report back this second time as I have had a completely different experience to that of last year. At the end of last year's seven weeks, I went away raving about how good it was and how much the students enjoyed it . . . This year, however, I feel that my maturity as an implementer of drama has really improved. I now clearly understand that drama is not just about acting and playing games but about accessing characters' feelings and emotions through exploration . . . I now view drama as an irreplaceable part of not only my literacy teaching but as my whole curriculum approach to teaching.

Works cited

Aubusson P, Ewing R & Hoban G (2009). *Action learning: reframing teacher professional development and learning*. London: Routledge.

Auerbach S (2012). *School leadership for authentic family and community partnerships*. New York: Routledge.

Australia Council for the Arts (2010). *More than bums on seats: Australian participation in the arts*. Sydney: Australia Council for the Arts.

Baldwin P (2012). *With drama in mind*. London: Continuum.

Baldwin P & Fleming K (2003). *Teaching literacy through drama: creative approaches*. London: Routledge Falmer.

Bamford A (2006). *The WOW factor: global compendium on the impact of the arts in education*. New York: Waxman.

Barkl L (2005). Professional musicians and interactive education programs: skills, knowledge and expertise required and implications for training. Paper presented at 'Backing our creativity: the national education and the arts symposium', Victorian College of the Arts, Melbourne, 12–14 September.

Bryce J, Mendelovits J, Beavis A, McQueen J, & Adams I (2004). *Evaluation of school-based arts education programmes in Australian schools*. Melbourne: Australian Council for Educational Research.

Bona M, Rinehart J & Volbrecht R (1995). 'Show me how to do like you': co-mentoring as feminist pedagogy. *Feminist Teacher*, 9(3): 116–24.

Burnaford G, Aprill A, & Weiss C (Eds) (2001). *Renaissance in the classroom: arts integration and meaningful learning*. New York: Routledge.

Caldwell B & Vaughan T (2012). *Transforming education through the arts.* London: Routledge.

Campbell V, Ewing R & Gibson R (2010). Evaluation of school drama pilot study. Unpublished report. Sydney: University of Sydney.

Catterall J (2009). *Doing well and doing good by doing art: the long term effects of sustained involvement in the visual and performing arts during high school.* Los Angeles: Los Angeles Imagination Group.

Cremin T, Mottram, E, Bearne M & Goodwin P (2008). Exploring teachers' knowledge of children's literature. *Cambridge Journal of Education*, 38(4): 449–464.

Deasy R (Ed) (2002). *Critical links: learning in the arts and student academic and social development.* Washington: Arts Education Partnership.

Dunn J & Stinson M (2011). Dramatic play and drama in the early years: Reimagining the approach. In S Wright (Ed.). *Children, meaning-making and the arts* (pp115–34). 2nd edn; Sydney: Pearson/Prentice-Hall.

Ewing R (Ed) (2012). *The creative arts in the lives of young children: play, imagination, learning.* Melbourne: Australian Council of Educational Research.

Ewing R (2010). *The arts and Australian education: realising potential.* Camberwell Vic.: Australian Council for Educational Research.

Ewing R (2006). Reading to allow spaces to play. In R Ewing (Ed.). *Beyond the reading wars: towards a balanced approach to helping children learn to read* (pp171–82). Sydney: Primary English Teaching Association.

Ewing R, Hristofski H, Gibson R, Campbell V & Robinson, A (2011). Using drama to enhance literacy: the School Drama initiative. *Literacy Learning: The Middle Years*, 19(3): 33–39.

Ewing R & Simons J (2004). *Beyond the script. Take two: drama in the classroom.* Sydney: PETA.

Fiske E (Ed) (1999). *Champions of change: the impact of the arts on learning.* Washington: Arts Education Partnership & President's Committee on the Arts and the Humanities.

Gibson R (2011). Evaluation of School Drama, 2010. Unpublished report. Sydney: University of Sydney.

Gibson R (2012). Evaluation of School Drama, 2011. Unpublished report. Sydney: University of Sydney.

Gibson R (2013). Evaluation of School Drama, 2012. Unpublished report. Sydney: University of Sydney.

Gibson R & Ewing R (2011). *Transforming the curriculum through the arts.* Melbourne: Palgrave Macmillan.

Gleeson L (2012). Why literature matters. In J Manuel & S Brindley (Eds.) *Teenagers and reading: literary heritages, cultural contexts and contemporary reading practices*. Kent Town, SA: Wakefield Press.

Le Cornu R (2005). Peer mentoring: engaging pre-service teachers in mentoring one another. *Mentoring and Tutoring*, 13(3): 355–66.

McCarthy K, Ondaatje E, Zakaras L & Brooks A (2004). *Gifts of the muse: reframing the debate about the benefits of the arts*. Santa Monica: RAND Corporation.

Miller C & Saxton J (2004). *Into the story: language in action through drama*. Portsmouth: Heinemann.

O'Connor P (2008). Drama for inclusion: a pedagogy of hope. In M Anderson, J Hughes & J Manuel (Eds.) *Drama and English teaching: imagination, action and engagement*. Melbourne: Oxford University Press

O'Neill C (1995). *Drama worlds: a framework for process drama*. Portsmouth, NH: Heinemann.

O'Toole J & Dunn J (2002). *Pretending to learn*. Sydney: Pearson.

President's committee on the arts and humanities (2011). *Reinvesting in arts education: Winning America's future through creative schools*. Washington: President's committee on the arts and humanities.

Robertson A (2010). The School Drama experience: a case study of learning English. Honours thesis: University of Sydney.

Upitis R (2005). Experiences of artists and artist-teachers involved in teacher professional development programs. *International Journal of Education & The Arts*, 6(8):1–11.

3
Drama and ecological understanding: stories of learning

David Wright

The teaching of drama occurs amidst conflict. All involved in the drama have a relationship to that conflict. And while conflict – within and between individuals and the circumstances in which they live – may appear to be ever present, it is also situated, systemic and subject to seemingly individual, unrelated and unexpected events. For these reasons conflict throws up opportunities for reflection, be they upon the process or the product of that conflict: drama. Frequently patterns of conflict can be seen – or found – and those patterns can also be seen to change over time in response to circumstance. Perceptions of this kind can be constructed as the basis of deeper ways of knowing and for this reason it is arguable that conflict is intimately related to learning and consciousness.

And while conflict can be identified and talked about, the naming of it always remains an interpretation: a phenomenon subject to language or 'languaging': the way we encounter the world through language (Maturana & Varela 1992). This interpretative element is even more evident when addressed through imagination, a principal reference in any artistic or creative endeavour (Courtney 1974) and embodiment (Wright 1998), the meaning made from sensed or felt experience.

Wright D (2015). Drama and ecological understanding: stories of learning. In M Anderson & C Roche (Eds). *The state of the art: teaching drama in the 21st century*, (49–66). Sydney: Sydney University Press.

This complex encounter includes but extends beyond improvisation (Hodgson & Richards 1977; Spolin 1983; Johnstone 1989), to place emphasis upon the reflective consciousness through which provisional and long-standing meaning is made. The drama experience therefore offers opportunities for depth and variety in human experience. It is in this depth and through this variety that the most insightful kinds of learning can arise.

Drama can be discussed therefore as a situated inquiry into conflict which gives rise to reflections which can challenge the assumptions upon which learning is based: a methodology that enables individual insight into social consciousness and the social construction of consciousness (Norris 2009). Necessarily, this needs to be tempered by acknowledgement that it is not drama per se that constructs these qualities but the effective facilitation or exploration of the repertoire of skills available in drama. Herein lies the responsibility of the drama educator: to ponder what he or she is attempting to do with the drama and why, and how and why the drama can be used to realise those goals. Drama, as much as and more than many discipline areas, requires the educator to have a sense of purpose beyond the provision of disciplinary knowledge and skills. Difficulties in articulating this have contributed to the vulnerability of the field. The capacity to facilitate drama as a method of knowing more than a method of showing is integral to its future.

In this chapter I use a series of very different stories to give a sense of ways in which 'ecological understanding' provides perspective upon learning. Equally, I look at the role of creative work in this process. Each story is one of relationships – be they personal, social, environmental and ideational – that give character to learning. The aim is to illuminate some of the complexities that can contribute to learning and the depth of understanding contained in an ecological perspective. Integral to each story is dramatic experience. Both drama skills and the skill of finding the drama in experience are relevant, as are settings within and outside of formal schooling. The focus is therefore on learning processes that lead to informed ways of living in a complex world. Hill, Wilson and Watson (2004) refer to this as 'learning ecology':

> Learning ecology provides a means for understanding and working with the complex and diverse ways in which individuals . . . learn, become more conscious, develop worldviews, change and act on their

values. It takes a constructivist view and acknowledges how our previous life experiences and opportunities, interactions, learning styles, and personalities result in each individual having a unique learning ecology (Hill et al. 2004, 49–50).

Drama, conflict and ecology

Because conflict is subject to ways in which it is known, it needs to be approached holistically: as something created by the interweaving of a multiplicity of elements. Some drama education theorists (e.g. Haseman & O'Toole 1989; O'Toole 1992) systematise this into the 'elements of drama' but my focus here is the whole rather than its constituent parts. The holistic is, in the words of Miller (1996), 'interrelated and dynamic'. This interrelationship becomes meaningful through, what Bateson calls, the 'pattern which connects' (Bateson 1988, 8). A variety of terms, as well as holistic, have been used to describe this form of pattern knowledge. Each suggests a particular orientation. They include 'integral' (Wilber 2007), 'systemic' (Ison 2010; Ramage & Shipp 2009) and 'ecological' (Bateson 1972, 1988; Capra 1996; Orr 1992). The focus in these orientations is both the integrated system and how the system is seen to be constructed: both ecology and ecological understanding. Equally, it is both the drama and the meaning that is made from the drama: the consciousness arrived at within and through the drama process. Clearly, drama cannot be encountered or interpreted apart from the systems of knowing and the environments within which the drama occurs. Patterns can be discerned and change arising from conflict is often central to these patterns: transition, transformation, construction, re-construction, emergence, revolution and revelation among them. All identify ways in which experience and understanding comingle in language and consciousness. Some patterns of change have been central to the history of drama (theatre and performance studies), principally personal or familial conflict. Other patterns of change appear to have only recently come to the fore (despite their longstanding presence). Conflict within and between humans and their environment have been with us for a long time but conflict arising from observations of environmental change over time – loss of biodiversity, global warming, rapid population growth, increased urbanisation and other issues arising from humankind's 'mastery' of its environment (Flannery 2010) – are a more recent phenomena. These changes are part of our life, they cannot be denied nor are they someone else's problem. Recognising this we must include ourselves, ecologically. As integral elements within this ecology we, the people, are integral to that change. We are embedded in the conflict and the opportunities for learning that arise as a result. Ecological change is our change. Questions about how we live within this conflict – how we learn in and through our relationship to challenges that are new to human experience – are key issues for educators of current and future generations. They cross all disciplines.

In this respect, ecological change is considerably more than a phenomenon of nature. It is many things to us. It is at the same time a consequence of scientific research, an opportunity for the affirmation of a social vision, a shadow over humanity's future, a symbol of our collective limitations, an avenue to seek out and affirm conspiracy, a means whereby a yearning for a mythical state can be called up and much more. It is a provocative challenge to the way we imagine and identify our futures. It initiates both perspective and phenomena, and both perspective and phenomena can be dreamed into and debated, hence their power. Such change has metaphoric significance, it is political and it is available dramatically (Lakoff & Johnston 1980; Lakoff 2002; Kershaw 2007). It is a story that can be told, re-told and re-told again, but effective storytelling requires learning. Such learning needs to tap into more than scientific research. It is led by the social learning that is at the heart of the conflict we encounter around unfolding circumstance. Joy, fear, frustration and the imagination of the community that lives within this are fundamental to its drama (Macy 1991). It is arguable therefore that issues of ecological imagination (Judson 2010), ecological literacy (Orr 1992; Capra 1996), ecological understanding (Bateson 1972, 1988; Harries-Jones 1995) and ecological intelligence (Bowers 2011) are integral to the design of education systems for a future encumbered by questions of ecological significance. Such issues require, Judson argues, 'a flexibility of mind oriented to interdependence and pattern, to the diversity and complexity that characterise natural and human-world relationships'. This type of process is 'inspired by one's emotional connection to the natural world. It can support our understanding of society, culture, reality and self in terms of relationship' (Bowers 2011,

3 Drama and ecological understanding

5). It is arguable therefore that the skills and understandings contained in creative processes like drama can be of great benefit in these sorts of activities.

The four very different stories that follow tell of dramatic practices that share a breadth of ambition. That ambition includes a desire to inculcate relationship. This is impossible to appreciate without some consideration of the extent to which the relationships we live in and through define our worldview. As these stories suggest, the laboratory of dramatic practice – be it a classroom, theatre, the world beyond or the imagination – is a formidable site for the study of the unfolding development of world views and the conflict such developments can give rise to.

First story: Korowal School

At 9.25 each morning Kindergarten, Year 1 and Year 2 students at Korowal School, a small independent non-systemic school in Sydney's Blue Mountains, gather with their teachers and those parents who have lingered after the morning drop-off and join in an elegantly designed example of ecological pedagogy, facilitated through an appreciation of the elements of drama.

Standing in a circle students, staff and parents perform a series of songs and poems that, in turn, acknowledge the new day, evoke respect for all students, situate the learning in a physical environment comprising animals and plants and other humans, and look forward to a rewarding day of interactive learning. This opening constructs a shared experience. Situated at the beginning of the day, it builds a platform for the future. It uses rhythm and emotion; it uses movement and group action. It seeks to connect directly with the values that motivate students in their relationships with the world around them. It is ritual learning that anticipates and supports the learning that is to follow. It begins with a short song.

> The bush is dancing in a ray of sunshine,
> the birds and animals are all at play,
> the world is breathing with the sound of daytime,
> wake up, welcome the day.

The state of the art

> Wake up (CLAP, CLAP),
> everybody wake up (CLAP, CLAP),
> wake up, welcome the day.

This is followed by a rhythmic poem, recited by all, that extends these sentiments. It begins . . .

> Good morning dear earth, good morning dear sun,
> good morning dear stones and flowers everyone,
> good morning to beasties and birds in the tree,
> good morning to you and good morning to me . . .

The third element, a circle-song performed with movement and often in rounds, celebrates those present. It begins . . .

> Circle of friends I love, let me tell you how I feel,
> You have given me such treasure,
> Circle round again . . .

This is followed by another brief poem, a minute of quiet and, a third poem beginning . . .

> Down is the earth and up is the sky, here are my friends and here am I . . .

The final element is a ritual 'Good morning' sung in turn by each staff member to the students and a ritual 'Good bye' sung to all parents still present.

Parents then shuffle from the room waving goodbye and blowing kisses. The staff takes command and the day moves forward.

This simple ritual can be seen as an example of the sort of education Bateson bemoaned the lack of, in his discussion of 'the pattern which connects'.

> Why do schools teach almost nothing of the pattern which connects?
> . . . What's wrong with them? What pattern connects the crab to the lobster and the orchid to the primrose and all four of them to me?

And me to you? And all six of us to the amoeba in one direction and to the back-ward schizophrenic in another? (Bateson 1988, 8)

It is through an appreciation of patterns in relationships that students are able to experience themselves in relation to learning subject matter. It is here that a depth of learning resides and it is here, within the construction and communication of relationships, that creative drama has the potential to excel. Without relationship, drama cannot exist.

The commencing ritual at Korowal School is a brief few minutes in an extended school day. From the point of view of an outsider who has observed this ritual, it introduces values and attitudes to the young children present. It requires teachers to model those values and attitudes. It is not an attempt to instill behaviours or provide answers. It indicates and communicates an approach to learning, developed over time, which contributes to the identity and orientation of the school. It is an attempt to draw children into connection with each other and the world beyond, and construct a sense of belonging. The design of an ecological education goes beyond acknowledging the complexity of interconnected life. It demands reflection upon the assumptions that inform daily existence.

Second story: at the University of Western Sydney – Drama Method class

Several years ago I introduced my Drama Method students to an exercise drawn from Heathcote's 'mantle of the expert' repertoire. This exercise imagines life in the shadow of a medieval monastery (Heathcote & Bolton 1995) as a means of interrogating social power. After discussing this model with my students it soon became apparent that none of my young Australian students lived in a village overlooked by a monastery. Very few Australians do. So we talked about that which did oversee our homes. One student, who lives in the nearby Blue Mountains – a vast undulating, forested world heritage area to the west of Sydney, separating the coastal fringe from the Western Plains – told us her home was overshadowed, especially each summer, by the strong possibility of bushfire. This became our subject matter and our drama playbuilding focused on our collective relationship to fire: its destructive power accompanied by its power to build community through adversity and its capacity to lay the ground for subsequent regeneration, regrowth and new life.

During an intense three-hour class we gathered tales of powerful visceral encounters with fire. These told of the fear of fire, the shock of its proximity, the piercing noise of warning sirens, the domination of the media by safety warnings, the red fire–smoke clouds that become the sky, the charred fragrance of burning eucalyptus followed some time later, after the danger has receded, by the return of bird life, the recovery of reptiles and the heartening sight and smell of new leaves sprouting fresh from charcoaled bark. These became the basis of our drama. The students who took part in the class encountered a deep, communal learning about fire, but more than this, their learning included an enhanced understanding of how their peers meet powerful existential challenge. It became an exercise in the building of community through vulnerability, trust and communication. Drama was the medium of the learning and fire the immediate subject matter but inter-relationship – intricate regional social and physical ecologies – were the substance of our class. 'I learned about fire as a collective experience,' said Denise. All in the class knew enough of bushfire to fear it as well as respect it enormously. All taught each other about their means of coping.

Third story: the deaf poet and sound

Aaron Williamson is a performance poet. He is also profoundly deaf, in a society that assumes hearing. The forms of knowledge constructed by Williamson's deafness are his principal poetic influence. For Williamson, his deafness is inescapable. It defines him ecologically. He lives within it and it is integral in the relationships that extend beyond. Consequently, he has chosen to invest the energy of his imagination into hearing. He knows that sound is something that he cannot know as hearing people do. Equally, he knows sound is something hearing people cannot know as he does – and by knowing in this way Williamson finds sound, for himself. It becomes essential to his learning. He writes of 'the sounds of words, trapped in the torso (that) continue with speaking. Silently.' And of being 'possessed by sounds . . . they have me . . . I

3 Drama and ecological understanding

feel them . . . I catch them before they reach out' and, 'The sickness itself, a language' (Williamson 1993, 24–25).

For Williamson sound rises up from the ground, into his legs, his pelvis then resonates between his diaphragm and his stomach. This is a sensation he has learned to 'hear'. It resonates alongside his own voice, which 'is something I experience primarily physically, through the jaw, in the chest etc. rather than in the site of the inner ear' (personal communication, 11 January 1995). Through the combination of his intelligence and his imagination this experience attains such clarity that the purpose of his writing and performance becomes, in part, his communication of that experience of sound. This can be confronting. Dyer describes his performance as a response to profound deafness mediated 'not by the use of conventional body language, but by a new and affective language of the body' (Dyer 1992, 113). Hutzulak (1994) describes it as work of 'feral intensity'. Almost inevitably, Williamson's dramatic pursuit of ways of representing and communicating a form of knowledge derived from isolation, self-absorption and 'otherness' can cause discomfort within his audience.

Necessarily, any attempt to represent Williamson's performance in words runs counter to his intent. Williamson not only seeks to, he needs to move beyond the verbal to imagine and give form to a means of communication that he becomes 'able-bodied' through. Williamson knows this systemically and ecologically.

> I'd . . . like to emphasise that my disability is not deafness . . . but speech as it is used by others and which disables me in terms of social exchange . . . Language literally fails us and yet, we have no other medium, no other direction to turn (personal communication, 1995).

The relationships through which Williamson arrives at language enable him to appreciate both creative expression and the limits of abstract reason. His frustration is accessible to all of us who have sought to understand something beyond our grasp. Herein lies the metaphor. Williamson's imagined relationship to sound connects me to my imagination of things I will never fully know. In truth, this is much of life. This illuminates a way of learning: of living with an aspiration to know. It is an essential ingredient of learning and it is the base from which all knowledge systems grow, along with the communities that live through them. It is implicit in the dramatic moment. In the embodied learning of Williamson the systemic base of social knowledge is made visible, to those able to encounter it. His dramatic relationship to it propels him to a form of understanding he might otherwise not obtain.

> 'the limits of language
> are the limits of our
> world'
> No. The limits of
> language are the limits
> of language.
> For here is the
> person before language.
> Not able, finally,
> to disappear. Capable
> of human form. (Williamson 1993, 67)

As Bateson reminds us, 'Ecology, in the widest sense ... (is) the interaction and survival of ideas and programs, (i.e. differences, complexes of differences etc.) in circuits' (Bateson 1972, 49). Literacy in this regard is, according to Orr, a 'quality of mind that seeks out connections' and is the opposite of the 'specialisation and narrowness characteristic of most education' (Orr 1992, 92).

Fourth story: encountering 'country'

The second Australian colloquium on 'sense of place' occurred at Hamilton Downs, a disused cattle station turned youth camp, 70 kms north-west of Alice Springs. This event was a dramatic encounter with a physical environment. Drama and performance are integral to knowledge of this place, and many places like it in parts of the continent not easily or usually accessed by non-Indigenous people. In a co-constructed piece of writing, co-ordinators of the colloquium, John Cameron and Craig San Roque sought to capture their thoughts on the event. In so doing they provided an introduction to their thinking on

3 Drama and ecological understanding

structuring learning in a non-traditional setting rich in interpretive and creative non-traditional learning methodologies.

> San Roque: In Australia, the country, or at least the Aboriginal country, is a seething mass of consciousness. Rocks, trees, watercourses, hills, ranges, all are impregnated with consciously held meanings, events, stories, all woven in intricate patterns of relationship and embodied in designs, song phrases and dance steps. This is a geographical literature which can be read once one has been taught the language and the perspective. Most of us who now live in Australia, and to some extent are the inheritors of this library, know of the existence of this inland sea of 'song lines' but are nevertheless profoundly unconscious of the subtle intimacy of the Creation Being's life and their role in keeping Aboriginal consciousness healthy and alert (Cameron & San Roque 2002, 77).

The ecology that contains the drama San Roque refers to is inescapable.

> Cameron: So, the interaction between Aboriginal and western senses of place must start from the recognition that Aboriginal people have a completely different conception of the relationship between consciousness and place to most Western people. Our first issue in designing the colloquium was how to bring out this difference, conceptually and experientially (77).

When I arrived at Hamilton Downs my initial response to the environment was surprise at its extraordinary diversity: the richness and variety of plant, insect and bird life, the array of colours and the unflinching power of the MacDonnell Ranges that dominate the view to the immediate south. This experience was enriched by the stories, told by ethno-botanist Peter Latz, of the watercourse that runs beneath the sandy riverbed that traverses the property and feeds the underground forest that peeks its branches above the red-brown earth. This and additional stories told by Latz and others, including Aboriginal custodian Bobby Stuart, gave more life to this seemingly harsh scrubland.

The majority of these stories were told in the opening sessions of the colloquium. A period described by Cameron as a 'day and a half of explanation of the depth of layering of Aboriginal stories of place, and why it isn't culturally appropriate or realistic to tell more than the outer layer to visiting white folk at the outset' (78). San Roque observed: 'Some of the group were powerfully moved by the end of [this day and a half], and understood they were in a different country in which different forces were at work on them'. He added, 'there are techniques and protocols for becoming accustomed to Aboriginal country and there are techniques [emerging] for recognising and decoding the communication from country' (79). Learning is driven by specific frames of reference when it is located in relationships of this complexity.

One of the methods used to decode learning was a 'morning dream circle'. San Roque said this 'was to enhance the participants' capacity to remain open and vulnerable to pre-conscious perceptions, to allow dream imagery to help in binding human consciousness to the place'. He situated this in traditional Aboriginal practice.

> 'It is the custom among some aboriginal groups to have what is often called in English "the morning news", when soon after waking, people will chatter, mutter and pass on the news from the night, this includes the news from dreams' (79–80).

Another of the methods used was gendered retreats and performances. For one day male and females separated and, under the guidance of locals, gathered to talk, sing, make music, dance and learn more about the region through ritual. This sought to acknowledge, among other things, the depth of difference in traditional male and female relationships to place, something traditionally marked in Aboriginal communities. This separation, over one day of walking, storytelling and ritual preparation, culminated in performances by the men for the women and by the women for the men: performances that contained and resulted in further stories – some of which are still told – within this locale.

In reflecting on the 'design' for the learning contained in the colloquium Cameron and San Roque wrote of the adaptive nature of the process. While Cameron argues the difficulties in containing the potentially deranging influence of country, San Roque argues the need to recognise the limits of human influence. 'Fortunately' he says, 'it [the design] wasn't just left to you and I. The country acts as both deranger and container'. Acknowledging this leads finally to acknowledgement of the role of country in learning. San Roque describes the colloquium as something arranged 'so that we could begin to think about such things in a place that still has the power to influence human being and human thought'. Cameron agrees. 'I have a feeling that although our planning and catalysing helped, it was the quality of this presence that was most important and most enduring. Perhaps this is one of the hallmarks of a social ecology' (88).

Imagination seems almost too soft a term to describe the construction of meaning when location is admitted as an educator. Here drama and imagination have constructed responsibility. This is reflected in the abiding importance of story, dream and drama. I remember most particularly a story told by Bobby Stuart in the final days of the colloquium, about the formation of a nearby section of the MacDonnell Ranges. His story depicted the ranges as a consequence of the interaction between mythological beings. And as he told the story I could see the story in the mountain range. I could read it in the rises and falls that he pointed to, in the outcrops and escarpments, in the ridges and valleys, in the wavering tensions of this fragile landscape. I could see this person chasing that person and at that place making camp. I could see the tension of the pursuit and the weapons and the old men and the young girl. I could see the place where the spear was thrown and the place of transformation where death gives birth to new life, which then becomes mythologised. This is the place where the story becomes the mountain range. In telling the story of the range the custodian tells the story of its coming into being. In maintaining the story, the custodian sustains the mountain range and the land in its vicinity and its creativity: its divinity. To the degree to which we share in it, it is our creativity, our drama as well: our cathedral, our text, our learning ecology embracing and encompassing us, to the degree to which we are able to admit it.

Implications for practice

The globalising, technologically based vision of learning that now dominates educational discourse places insufficient emphasis on localised and embodied aspects of learning. The enactment of this vision has often been to the detriment of arts-based learning. This is despite the fact that creative insight into the interdependent relationship between individuals, societies, environments, technologies and belief systems are integral to an arts-based education and our students' informed participation in our unfolding future.

Those innovative practitioners interested in exploring the vast range of knowledge and skills implicit in drama learning can enrich basic understanding through focus upon localised, embodied learning, in part through reference to the complex web of relationships through which knowledge is constructed. A systemic worldview draws attention to the many variables that determine consciousness. This is why drama, in the hands of thoughtful, sensitive and creative facilitators, is an exciting arena for this sort of work. The dramatic moment, when given due attention, can be seen to exist within an extraordinarily rich nest of relationships, each capable of turning the moment one way or another. All involved in that moment should be attuned to its possibilities and open to reflection upon them.

In practice, the drama student must be encouraged to consider his or her relationship to the self, as moderator of the encounter; to the character as part of the means by which an alternate reality is constructed; to other participants – as individuals, as bodies, as skilled performers, as avenues or impediments, as rhythms, as aesthetic forms, as characters, as integral in a process of dramatic development; to the environment – both natural and constructed, both within the space and beyond; to design – in body, body arrangement, costume, pattern, colour, shading, shape, setting; to technology – in-built and/or effects created as required; to musicality – in tone of speech and composition; to audience – as sharing participants in the suspension of reality, as fellow travellers in a dramatic journey, critical observers, as customers, as friends or family, as co-participants in a changing world, as examiners perhaps; to context – the educational-social-political-cultural-ecological encounter with life within which this creative construction unfolds, and more. All these, plus key decision or choices that have lead to the strategic and/or inadvertent encounter with these elements. And of course the overall phenomenological experience. How it felt in the moment of its occurrence. How it feels now, some time after the event. What lingers; what is forgotten.

In the context of drama this can be seen as a subset of the vast array of encounters that determine consciousness. Alternately it can be seen as a powerful exercise in entering into this vast array (and thereby opening up to this potential). The limits to consideration here, to imagination, insight and understanding, can be as critical as the creative choices made at any stage of the process. Here educators have the responsibility to open to possibility rather than to close to truth. All decisions of this kind construct a basis for further action: 'all doing is knowing; all knowing is doing' (Maturana & Varela 1992, 27).

This mapping of the web of relationships is a practical exercise often used in environmental studies to help individuals position themselves in relation to the interweaving elements that sustain life. It is an approach that has a place in drama. Identifying, indeed mapping the networks that sustain performance challenges practitioners to enter deeply into the relationships that sustain individual and collective roles.

A systemic worldview requires that individual teachers reflect upon their participation in their learning and that of their community. This requires that the teacher understands him or herself as a participant in the reflection that facilitates learning and that this reflection be accepted as an experience of learning with significance for all in the community of learners (of which the teacher is only one). Out of this arises an ethical responsibility to act upon that learning.

> Becoming aware of one's awareness and understanding one's understanding gives rise to a feeling of responsibility for what one is doing, for what one is creating .. Once this has been understood, one cannot pretend any longer to be unaware of one's understanding ... it is not understanding that entails responsibility but the knowledge of knowledge (Maturana cited in Poerksen 2004, 52).

This sort of learning has the potential to transform the assumptions that construct attitudes and actions. Work in transformative learning expands on that potential (Taylor, et al. 2012).

> Transformative learning involves experiencing a deep, structural shift in the basic premises of thought, feeling and action. It is a shift of consciousness that dramatically and permanently alters our way of being in the world. Such a shift involves our understanding of ourselves and our self-locations; our relationships with other humans and with the natural world; our understanding of relations of power in interlocking structures of class, race and gender; our body-awarenesses; our visions of alternative approaches to living; and our

sense of possibilities for social justice and peace and personal joy (O'Sullivan et al. 2002, xviii).

Essential to transformation of this kind is story. In the words of Gregory Bateson:

> There is a story which I have used before and shall use again: A man wanted to know about mind, not in nature, but in his private large computer. He asked it (no doubt in his best Fortran), 'Do you compute that you will ever think like a human being?' The machine then set to work to analyse its own computational habits. Finally, the machine printed its answer on a piece of paper, as such machines do. The man ran to get the answer and found, neatly typed, the words: 'that reminds me of a story' (Bateson 1988, 13).

Conclusion

In all the stories told in this chapter, some of which are more easily translated to drama education practice than others, locality, embodiment and relationship are central. Each is a story of relational learning. All are located quite specifically, in focused experience. That focus can be driven by specific events. This is not abstract knowledge, it is grounded and yet it carries relevance to a variety of setting and situations outside of that being discussed. Thomas Berry's argument, in his foreword to Edmund O'Sullivan's treatise on the transformation required for an emerging 'ecozoic' era, is worth citing here;

> Every profession and occupation of humans must establish itself within the integral functioning of the planet. The earth is the primary teacher in economics, in medicine, in law, in religion. Earth is the primary educator. Ecology is not a part of economics. Economics is an extension of ecology (O'Sullivan 1999, xiv).

In this respect drama education can be seen as a laboratory for the ongoing exploration of participation in unfolding awareness. Accordingly, one of the principal functions of an education in drama is insightful pursuit of understanding and the circumstances that facilitate that understanding.

If drama is an education in the employment of conscious awareness, this awareness affirms the way in which drama facilitates 'more than drama', because ecological understanding is certainly 'more than drama'. Employed skillfully, drama processes have the capacity to enable an enriched awareness of the numerous relationships in which we participate. This underpins all arguments for drama as an epistemological form, with particular relevance to ecological understanding. In presenting this discussion this chapter has looked at a series of sites, practices and learning experiences and suggested questions about how and why these practices place so much importance on creative responses to individual, social and ecological encounter.

Works cited

Bateson G (1972). *Steps to an ecology of mind*. New York: Ballantine Books.
Bateson G (1988). *Mind and nature*. New York: Bantam Books.
Bowers CA (2011). *Perspectives on the ideas of Gregory Bateson, ecological intelligence, and educational reform*. Eugene, OR: Eco-Justice Press.
Cameron J & San Roque C (2002). Coming into country: the catalysing process of social ecology, In *PAN (Philosophy, Activism, Nature)* 2: 76–88.
Capra F (1996). *The web of life* London: Harper Collins.
Courtney R (1974). *Play, drama and thought*. London: Cassell.
Dyer R (1992). The anatomy of utterance; the poetry and performance of Aaron Williamson. In S Dwyer (ed). *Rapid eye 2*. London: Annihilation Press.
Flannery T (2010). *Here on Earth*. Melbourne: Text Publishing.
Harries-Jones P (1995). *A recursive vision: ecological understanding and Gregory Bateson*. Toronto: University of Toronto Press.
Haseman B & O'Toole J (1989). *Dramawise*. Melbourne: Heinemann Education.
Heathcote D & Bolton G (1995). *Drama for learning*. London: Heinemann.
Hill SB, Wilson S & Watson, K (2004). Learning ecology: a new approach to learning and transforming ecological consciousness. In E O'Sullivan & M Taylor. *Learning towards an ecological consciousness*. New York: Palgrave Macmillan.
Hodgson J & Richards E (1977). *Improvisation*. London: Methuen
Hutzulak C (1994). Holythroat: an interview with Aaron Williamson. *Filling Station Magazine*. April 1994: 9–12.

Ison R (2010). *Systems practice: how to act in a climate-change world*. Milton Keynes: Open University & Springer.
Johnstone K (1989). *Impro*. London: Methuen.
Judson G (2010). *A new approach to ecological education*. New York: Peter Lang.
Kershaw B (2007). *Theatre ecology*. Cambridge: Cambridge University Press.
Lakoff G (2002). *Moral politics*. Chicago: University of Chicago Press.
Lakoff G & Johnston M (1980). *Metaphors we live by*. Chicago: University of Chicago Press.
Macy J (1991). *World as lover, world as self*. Berkeley CA: Parallax Press.
Maturana HR & Varela FJ (1992). *The tree of knowledge*. Boston: Shambhala.
Miller JP (1996). *The holistic curriculum*. Toronto: OISE Press.
Norris J (2009). *Playbuilding as qualitative research*. Walnut Creek, CA: Left Coast Press.
Orr D (1992). *Ecological literacy*. Albany, NY: SUNY Press
O'Sullivan E (1999). *Transformative learning*. London: Zed Books.
O'Sullivan E, Morrell A & O'Connor M (2002). *Expanding the boundaries of transformative learning*. New York: Palgrave.
O'Toole J (1992). *The process of drama*. London: Routledge.
Poerksen B (2004). *The certainty of uncertainty*. Exeter, UK: Imprint Academic.
Ramage M & Shipp K (2009). *Systems thinkers*. Milton Keynes & London: Open University & Springer.
Spolin V (1983). *Improvisation for the theater*. Evanston IL: Northwestern University Press.
Taylor EW, Cranton P & Associates (2012). *The handbook of transformative learning*. San Francisco: Jossey-Bass.
Wilber K (2007). *The integral vision*. Boston: Shambhala.
Williamson A (1993). *A holythroat symposium*. London: Creation Press.
Wright D (1998). Embodied learning: approaching the experience of the body in drama education. *NADIE Journal NJ*, 22(2): 87–95.

4
Schooling the imagination in the 21st century . . . (or why playbuilding matters)

Christine Hatton and Sarah Lovesy

Playbuilding has been a constant focus, particularly in NSW, in terms of formal drama curriculum in schools. Learning about drama by doing drama is at the core of drama syllabus documents within Australia and in numerous other countries. Drama pedagogy centres around the artistic practice of the art form, enabling students to 'learn about' the art form as they 'learn to' negotiate drama as artists. In drama, experiential learning is key as students collaborate and embody their learning through role-play, performance and critique. The 'live' experience of making, performing and appreciating the drama work is critical to building students' foundational understandings of the subject. Playbuilding has been a central feature of NSW syllabus documents for over 20 years now, as a core or compulsory context for study, where students from K–12 learn how to create their own original plays. The prominence of playbuilding in NSW drama curriculum has in turn enabled teachers to hone their practice and develop sophisticated pedagogy and approaches to assessment and examination in this area. Surprisingly, however, there is little research that captures this pedagogy in action and describes its nuances and learning benefits, from a drama or a general education point of view. This chapter will describe and theorise

Hatton C & Lovesy S (2015), 'Schooling the imagination in the 21st century ... (or why playbuilding matters)'. In M Anderson & C Roche, (Eds). *The state of the art: teaching drama in the 21st century*, (67–83). Sydney: Sydney University Press.

the practice of playbuilding in the drama classroom and will position playbuilding pedagogy centrally within the current discourses of 21st-century learning.

These are tumultuous times for education. Late modernity presents many challenges for educators; the shifts and demands of economic crises, globalisation, ecological and social change and the impact of ubiquitous technologies are all critical forces that are shaping the way schooling is done around the world. Various contemporary educationalists and researchers would argue that considering the precarious future we face, education and schooling need to change dramatically to meet what we guess might be ahead (Kalantzis & Cope 2005; New London Group 1996; Heppell 2012; Robinson 2011). There is a growing chorus of educational leaders, researchers, and communities calling for a radical shake up in the way we 'do' school in the 21st century and they argue that there is an urgent need to revise buildings, pedagogies and approaches to curriculum to cater for 21st-century learners.

In the knowledge or learning age of the 21st century, learners' needs have changed while education systems and decision-makers are slow to act and transform systems and approaches (Heppell 2012; Prensky 2006; Wagner 2008). Our school systems and thinking remain locked in the outmoded industrial past and misguidedly focus on standardised testing, regimes of accountability and risk management rather than the real (and possibly expensive) work of preparing schools, teachers and learners for a complex and difficult future. There is continuing discussion around the need for a rethink about what pedagogical reforms need to occur. Much of this rhetoric adopts an arts flavour as prominent educationalists and commentators speak of the critical need for creative capacity-building to be at the heart of future-oriented education and learning (Robinson 2011; Heppell 2012; Pink 2005).

While there is much in these discussions and debates that resonate with drama educators and give some hope (i.e. 'at last they are talking about what we know'), the absence of drama and the arts in providing clear evidence of these creative pedagogies in action is nevertheless seriously concerning. Good drama pedagogy is, as O'Toole argues, perhaps the most productive pedagogy of all (2002). However, the arts are rarely used as models of excellence when it comes to pedagogies of the future. While at political and system levels there is new interest in creativity capacity-building for the future, there is still some reticence by the wider education field to acknowledge the many and varied ways drama and the arts already do this kind of work. Drama has concrete processes, methods and forms to develop these 21st-century skills and understandings that are now so highly prized. This chapter seeks to redress the absence of drama within these wider debates by framing drama, and specifically playbuilding pedagogy, within the context of these calls for dynamic 21st-century pedagogies that cater for flexible, risk-taking, creative student collaborators. Drama learning processes cut to the core of these attributes and exemplify much of the rhetoric of 21st-century pedagogies.

There is continuing discussion around the needs of 21st-century learners and the shift from old content-driven approaches in education to more fluid, 'child-led' (Heppell 2012) approaches where the learner is actively engaged as a content creator, learning the skills to manoeuvre across disciplines and using varied tools in a range of spaces, both real and virtual. There have been increasing calls for learning to be more like a game (Gee & Levine 2009; Barab et al. 2009), where end-focused creative play is a necessary part of the learning and inquiry process. While drama education has been reasonably slow to engage with ICT and to integrate technologies into creative processes, many of the creative, playful learning processes and ways of working in drama offer clear evidence of 21st-century attributes in action. Drawing on the input of business leaders, Tony Wagner (2008) outlines some of these 21st-century skills in his book, *The global achievement gap*:

- critical thinking and problem solving
- collaboration across networks and leading by influence
- agility and adaptability
- initiative and entrepreneurialism
- effective oral and written communication
- accessing and analysing information
- curiosity and imagination.

Repeatedly, notions of playfulness, creative thinking and collaboration feature heavily throughout much of the literature on 21st-century learning (Pink 2005). Erica McWilliam's publications on creative capacity-building and cognitive playfulness are analogous with the open creative processes of the drama classroom and playbuilding in particular (McWilliam 2008; Tan & McWilliam 2009). In playbuilding processes where knowledge is assembled and performed on the workshop floor, and where playfulness is a critical part of the collaborative process of devising, students are engaging directly in and developing the kinds of learning dispositions that are considered most necessary in a future-oriented learning process. Tan and McWilliam see play as a 'multiliteracy' for 21st-century life and work (2009, 1). Similarly Cope and Kalantzis's (2009) theories of multimodal multiliteracies take in many of the modalities playbuilders work with to construct original embodied artworks for performance:

- written language
- oral language
- visual representation
- audio representation
- tactile representation
- gestural representation
- representation to oneself
- spatial representation.

In playbuilding processes learners are engaged in complex forms of representation for specific theatrical purposes and audiences, where play and playfulness is a necessary part of the devising process. They independently create the work at hand and negotiate dramatic elements, as well as the complexities of self as a collaborator, responding to context and working with specific frames of dramatic form.

Theorising playbuilding in action

To understand the connections between playbuilding and 21st-century learning, it is important to first theorise and describe the nature of the playbuilding learning process. Playbuilding is a unique drama method involving drama teachers working with groups of students to devise and perform their own plays from their group's imagination. Through playbuilding, students can investigate, shape and symbolically represent ideas, feelings, attitudes and their consequences. It is a creative process that has rich possibilities for learning as it gives students a powerful means to share their views with others in the community. For groups of students undertaking a playbuilding project, ideas need 'to be given flesh and blood and emotional reality: [and] it must go beyond imitation' (Brook 1993, 9). The essence of playbuilding is for the group to explore ways for their imaginative ideas to be re-invented, to be fresh and new, or perhaps challenging and ultimately to give their ideas dramatic substance. It is a transformative educational process at work. The playbuilding group creates its own dynamics while undertaking this process and product journey, as playbuilding encourages a cooperative approach to exploring the world through enactment. Therefore the collaborative nature of playbuilding enables students to engage in a creative process of sharing, developing and expressing ideas. The form can also help students transform their knowledge and engage in reflection and criticism as it is through the context of group inquiry in playbuilding that a student may reach a 'greater critical knowing about her/his actions and how they are informed and influenced' (Smith & Lovat 1991, 77). Playbuilding allows groups of students to enter and experience imagined worlds collectively and collaboratively. These imaginative worlds begin at the start of the process when playbuilders are given the opportunity to enter into an experiential learning phase which operates through playing and improvising.

The importance of playing and improvising

It is valuable to explore the connections between 'playing' and 'improvising' in playbuilding in order to glimpse the connections between the affective, cognitive and physical domains of learning. As drama educators, we know that drama students love to play (Lovesy 2004, 23); playing games with rules and consequences, playing with ideas, playing with spontaneous and structured improvisation, and playing with various theatre conventions and techniques. Playing and improvising brings freedom to students' imaginations, creativity and instincts, and helps them grow effectively; it enables students to discover meaning in the world, and this opens up spaces for creativity and intuition; meaning and understanding therefore become part of the experience (Winnicott 1971, 41). Play and improvisation, whether created informally by students or in a more formal drama games structure, creates dialectical moments, the winners and the losers, the tagged and the free, the excitement and the disappointment, the rules and the subrules. The players are playing in a dual world; in some sense they are exploring the actual and fictional worlds within their games and activities. These kinds of classroom activities have critical benefits for the learner that can strengthen their confidence and sense of identity. In Christine Hatton's doctoral research (2005) on student learning in playbuilding processes she found that the girls in her study relished the experience of exercising control over the drama and character's emotions. Experimenting in this way through role and performance, where the students had artistic control over the dramatic structure and performance event, gave them important opportunities to be visible and in charge of their learning. Knowledge and skill (about self, dramatic artistry, story and context) are performative in playbuilding projects and represent significant 'acts' of learning.

Improvisation is a major teaching and learning tool which begins the playbuilding process as it allows freedom of student expression and movement. The spontaneity inherent in any type of improvisation activity can minimise the number of students trying to imitate other people's ideas and give the students freedom to explore their own ideas. Spontaneity in improvisation can be inspiring as thoughts and actions not previously dreamt about come alive. Improvisation creates a group curiosity, where the group's ideas can be examined closely in a non-threatening environment. Improvisation is practical and provocative; practical as it is played out on the classroom floor allowing students to develop their personal techniques and skills, and provocative because it taps into the untold potential of the students which awakens intuition. Viola Spolin argues that intuition, in improvisation, transcends the limitation of the familiar and responds to immediacy – the right now. Intuition comes bearing its gifts in the moment of spontaneity when the person is free to relate and act in the changing dramatic world (Spolin 1963, 3–5). Improvisation is used to release the potential of not just the individual but the group, and is an organic means of releasing imaginative intuition that underpins the group's process work. Playbuilding is built upon these foundations and as such it can be ambiguous and move in several directions at once in the classroom. In this environment the group can change the rules, create tensions, and use their collective energy to provoke ideas within their collective imaginings. In Sarah Lovesy's doctoral research she discovered that if a playbuilding group can release a dramatic immediacy and intuition in their playing and improvising, then the firing of students' imaginations starts to take place. In turn, this allows playbuilding groups to work together with enjoyment, to take dramatic risks, to manage and solve problems and to step into their initial exploration of devising a story (Lovesy 2004).

Schooling the imagination through playbuilding

Imagining is a dynamic process that belongs to the conscious and subconscious. Awakening the imagination belongs to the realm of emotions, imagery, memory, and is a state of mind and body (Greene 1995, 28). The imagination's 'imaginings' are curious and inquisitive and can be transformed.

Playbuilding students use their own unique imaginations to explore the visual, verbal and non-verbal ideas in their learning. They often create their own theatrical language through muscular and emotional classroom activities. In the initial stages of playbuilding the students share with one another their previous drama and theatre knowledge and observations, and hence their imaginings. Although they can create this information in a variety of ways, the individual observations and imaginings are tied to their perceptions of the world. Each student's belief in the topics or issues chosen for playbuilding informs another students' perceptions. This 'informing' can provide a dramatic tension as members of the group may have different perspectives depending whether they perceive through looking, seeing or doing. This tension arises from letting the imagination run freely, and the group eventually forms its own group perceptions. These in turn flow into the devising and, as such, there is a complexity in the imaginative and creative processes that power the students' work (Lovesy, 2004).

In a playbuilding project, imaginative complexity comes from the range of students' interests, levels and abilities, and in any given class there may be what some drama educators call 'super-dramatists' (Dunn 1996, 21). Betty Jane Wagner clarifies this notion of the super-dramatist, arguing that in a drama class the teacher can find students intuitively leading the dramatic action. These super-dramatists are providing a framework upon which other students can build a new understanding (Wagner 1995, 68). The drama teacher's role is to create an environment where super-dramatists can be extended, while still providing a dynamic learning experience for students who do not have the same level of ability.

Playbuilding groups have the capacity to construct multiple realities within their conceptual networks as they explore the potential for transforming. Transformation is inherent in the drama process, as is the process of imagination which 'utilises affective states and intuition in its functioning' (Burton 1991, 172). Maxine Greene says that 'transformative pedagogies must relate both to existing conditions and to something we are trying to bring into being, something that goes beyond a present situation' (1995, 1); here she is analysing the power of the imagination. Similarly, Bruce Burton believes that 'imagination is a potent element in learning because it permits the individual to transform experience and transcend the limits of what is already known' (1991, 172). Burton further notes that drama is essentially a creative experience, and 'creativity is a universal and complex element of human behavior which is significant in a whole range of learning experiences' (Burton 1991, 173). These ideas encompass the concept that imaginative and creative experiences generate and transform the playbuilding process though 'illuminating, extending and enhancing ... learning' (Burton 1991, 176). In playbuilding, drama students collaborate within this imaginative and creative experience.

Metaphoric transformation

A metaphor is an active mode through which to experience drama ideas symbolically. It is another way of transforming the imaginative and creative energies in playbuilding. Moore and Yamamoto describe metaphor as a way to transfer bodily meaning; they say that metaphor creates 'a new context and configuration of meanings, thus becoming not merely a poetic device, but a whole new way of thinking about the world' (Moore & Yamamoto 1988, 29). Students need to understand not only what a metaphor is but how it affects their thinking. Through this effect students can be encouraged to creatively explore information and knowledge and to 'highlight certain features', and to 'suppress or hide certain features' (Moore & Yamamoto 1988, 30) in their devising. When playbuilders engage in metaphoric work it provides a contextual framework and gives rise to new modes of interpretation, allowing students to see ideas in a new light, hence metaphors both amplify and diminish the human experience.

Metaphoric imaginative thought and action can provide rich possibilities for students learning more about their work, and it is an important property in playbuilding which enables students to catch the essence of their group stories. It can give playbuilding its dramatic power, as metaphor exists through the embodiment of the physical, cognitive and affective domains of the students. Students can be encouraged actively to be responsible for their own metaphoric devising in the drama aesthetic, and this can occur when the students are engaged in opening their minds and feelings. A metaphor allows students to extend their knowing so that they have the opportunity to layer and broaden the inner and outer life of their fictional work. The metaphoric world of the idea can be expanded within the minds and imaginations of the students through practical experiences in the drama classroom (Moore & Yamamoto 1983). For instance, in drama, students may wish to transform themselves into an anthropomorphic idea; in this case they will endow their ideas with symbolic and metaphoric life.

In playbuilding, students explore metaphoric creating so that they understand, use and interpret their own examples. Students may approach this through verbal imagery, and through the creation of visual metaphors with their bodies. Helping groups to select and emphasise imagery in words and phrases and to use their physicality entails experimentation and failure. This experimentation and failure allows a creative freedom for students to explore their own as well as other students' imaginations. Metaphor, imagining, devising and creating can be fused together in drama education, allowing metaphoric osmosis to take place.

Elements of drama

All drama learning is informed and shaped by students' understandings of the elements of drama and their skills in using these on the floor and in performance. Haseman and O'Toole provide a useful model of the art form and the way its elements convey dramatic meaning:

The human context (situations, roles, relationships) driven by dramatic tension directed by focus made explicit in place & time through language & movement to create mood & symbols which together create the whole experience of dramatic meaning. (1986, viii)

When we think about playbuilding processes other elements can be added to this model such as:

- *Audience engagement* which is integral to students understanding the purpose and meaning of their playbuilding project.
- *Characterisation* as there is a need to differentiate between role and character in playbuilding; role work involves students representing and identifying with a particular set of circumstances, whereas characterisation involves students in the process of developing a fully realised character from their role.
- *Dramatic moments* which are fundamental to helping students to understand that a number of moments make up scenes, and each separate moment is pivotal to developing and building the dramatic tension.
- *Student focus* which needs to be continually nurtured and developed throughout every project.

As students become more expert dramatists and playbuilders they learn from their embodied experiences and gradually become more adept and independent when using the elements of drama in their work. When students are improvising leading to playbuilding they manipulate these elements for effect and impact, communicating their ideas through their selective use of the various elements. In playbuilding, students should have a range of different opportunities to play with the elements of drama in different combinations so they can consider the ways in which the elements are working to achieve their dramatic purpose and impact. Different types of playbuilding processes may involve students emphasising particular elements for a specific style or purpose (e.g. a heightened use of symbol in non-realist or abstract forms and styles).

Every activity and playbuilding process should involve students experimenting with the elements in practical ways and also critically reflecting on the way the elements are working at any given point in their drama work. Discussing the elements of drama during the devising process offers opportunities for rich discussion about the art form and the way students are using it. Teachers can focus on the elements of drama in the way they structure activities, as well as self or peer evaluation processes. This encourages students to develop their critical thinking skills and their ability to respond to the live and dynamic experience of the drama as both a participant and as an audience member (Hatton & Lovesy 2009).

Learning through metaxis

Drama educators use the term 'metaxis' to describe the interplay between the actual and the fictitious in the drama classroom. Metaxis appears to have an elusive quality, as the notion of 'interplay' can vary in degrees among groups of students and teachers. Bruce Burton explains the importance of metaxis by proposing that the 'drama process requires a special act of the imagination, effectively defined by Augusto Boal as metaxis' (Burton 1991, 7). Burton argues:

> 'for the drama process to occur, and create the interplay of metaxis which can lead to insight, certain essential elements of experience must be present. These elements are: imagination, creativity, identification, transformation and discovery' (Burton 1991, 8).

Metaxis is a term that is intangible, yet definable, as it exists as an integral part of the drama education process, and hence playbuilding.

Metaxis reciprocates between both the 'real and the fictional' worlds, or in other words the duality between the 'actual and fictitious', is explored. This duality is examined not only through the students' playbuilding, but also through the exchange between teacher and students in the drama experience. Metaxis helps drama teachers and students alike to comprehend drama aesthetics and dramatic meaning. It is therefore like the 'subtexts' (O'Toole 1992, 75) of the drama class, where words, images, ideas, knowledge, physicality, feelings, conscious and unconscious imaginings occur simultaneously. This capacity of drama teachers and students to hold two worlds simultaneously in their minds and bodies in the drama classroom implies that metaxis underplays the work being carried out by everyone in the class.

Metaxis is connected to the liminal (Turner 1982), in that the liminal can be visualised as a space that makes way for new ideas yet still connects to the old ideas. A liminal period of time refers to when 'the actual work of rites of passage takes place' (Schechner 2002, 57), and hence a liminal transformation occurs when students enter this period of time. The concept of liminal is therefore embedded in metaxis and the rituals of a playbuilding classroom. A drama group's playbuilding has a particular kind of being in-between the actual and fictitious worlds, a 'metaxis which feeds into the drama' (O'Toole 1992, 220) so that the body, mind, and environment can be connected willingly within the imaginative moment; this could be described as metaxical embodiment.

In playbuilding the dual affect of the actual and the fictional can provide a tension in the space between the two worlds that occur in the classroom. An example of this is when a playbuilding group is discussing, debating and improvising ideas to begin the playbuilding process. At this time students are continually working in their actual world, but tapping into the fictional world; their ideas sometimes work and sometimes they don't. Sometimes ideas that seemed significant in group discussion break down in the fictional improvisation, and ideas that seemed insignificant in the group discussion may come to life in the fictional improvisation; this is metaxical embodiment at work. It incorporates the tension of the two colliding worlds, and produces experiences that give the playbuilders a passage into embodiment.

Warren Linds connects metaxis to embodiment, arguing that:

> The two worlds of metaxis in ourselves are autonomous. Metaxis occurs in the artist's body and is embodied. Self and mind are woven through the entire human body and through the web of the relationships in which that self takes shape. (Linds 1998, 74)

Therefore it is through the process of metaxis that playbuilding becomes the interplay between the imagined and the actual, the tangible and the ephemeral. Metaxis is like an invisible film over playbuilding practice.

4 Schooling the imagination in the 21st century

Playbuilding as a pedagogy for the future

As an 'artful' pedagogy, playbuilding requires a repertoire of artistic practice and skills of drama teachers and students. Teachers must support students' creative processes as they weave the elements of form to create dramatic meanings that are their own. The skills and understandings dynamised within the playbuilding process cross over into skills and multiliteracies necessary for living in the 21st-century. Teachers artfully create the contexts and processes for students to engage in playbuilding projects that can have lasting outcomes for learners. The teacher must expertly construct, guide and manage the devising process as it happens. In doing so they must consider: what will be the school drama moments that may profoundly affect them in the future, and how can they teach this form to create evocative thinking, doing and purposeful imaginative engagement in the arts?

Sue Davis argues for teachers to unpack what creativity might mean in drama teaching and learning in the 21st-century and states that more students tend to believe that drama work such as playbuilding was the most creative kind of drama (Davis 2010, 39). Roslyn Arnold's theories on educating for empathic intelligence are a dynamic teaching model that explores human emotions in the drama classroom. She explores the interpersonal engagements in a classroom that facilitate student-centred pedagogy and argues that the development of empathy in a teacher 'requires, and indeed helps us to develop a nonjudgmental stance in our responses to human behaviour' (Arnold 2000, 6). She asserts that 'Empathy is an act of heartfelt, thoughtful imagination' (Arnold 2000, 7) and through calling it an 'act' indicates that emotion involves affect as well as cognition. An empathic drama teacher will stress the special devising nature of playbuilding which necessitates a high level of trust between participants because of that very special, personal and imaginative creating that occurs. An empathic learning environment enables playbuilders to create their own unique diverse imaginations, thereby opening up a myriad of creative possibilities in the drama learning space. A playbuilding group's imagination is being tried, tested, re-arranged and shifted through the teaching that occurs. Furthermore, the groups and individual students within them, continue to advance their learning when teaching is attuned to their needs (Arnold, 1998, 2000). This is 'artful' pedagogy.

Joe Winston discusses how teachers might foster a vision for arts education in which the social values this learning embodies are as important as the appearance of the final creative product. He believes that this type of arts education values the creative energies of students in a way that allows them to channel understanding of their communal world, and their own individual creativity (Winston 2010, 86–108). He also argues for the pedagogic importance of a final creative product stating that for students who love performing 'there is nothing quite so thrilling as the moment when their work is shared, watched and/or listened to' (Winston 2010, 76). This sharing with an audience creates a sense of aesthetic necessity which develops and guides the students' reflections, decisions and evaluations of the creative process. Joe Winston's arguments relate directly to why playbuilding is a pedagogy for the future as they demonstrate the educational importance of drama process work combined with the actor/audience relationship.

Ken Robinson (2011) proposes that 21st-century education should focus on helping students to become creative thinkers and doers, as we are now living in a cultural and social revolution, a tumultuous time of change, an extraordinary complex world that demands new skills, knowledge and understanding. This means that education should become personalised as 21st-century students may not know what they are capable of unless given the opportunity – we all have a different sense of possibility. By equally valuing the educational potential of the arts, with its convergence on creativity and helping students to explore their imaginative capacities, teachers can create classrooms that focus on learning without frontiers. Arts education is at the centre of this dynamic conception of a revolution in education. In a playbuilding classroom these theorists and educators ideas have the potential to 'play' a central role in the learning that takes place.

Conclusion

In our NSW curriculum some of what goes on in the classroom works against playbuilders' imaginations as education systems and authorities have an obsession with assessment, evidence and benchmarks. The act of imagining is connected to students' creativity through transformation and this transformation links directly to exploration, experience and discovery in the drama classroom. Yes, this can be assessed and examined but at what costs? How do we assess or examine playfulness and risk-taking in terms of dramatic form in a contemporary sense? Are our curriculum constraints and imperatives in fact limiting the innovative practice of teachers and students? Playbuilding promotes relationships with theatre practitioners, relationships that can encourage drama students to examine and connect with the artistry of others. In addition, playbuilding projects engage with traditions, stories and communities, often where students are working in interdisciplinary ways and using research dynamically within their dramatic choices in the work. This in turn means that students are exploring the imaginations and creativity of others and developing a wider self-expression through their cognitive, affective and physical selves in dialogue with others and other contexts. In this way playbuilding projects provide creative spaces for personal engagement and empowerment as students position and situate themselves and their creative practice within wider issues and communities of artists. Importantly, playbuilding enables young people to engage in big picture issues and stage their own stories.

The collaborative playbuilding learning process described here resonates with models of 21st-century learning. Playbuilding projects provide learners with critical opportunities to develop personal meaning, creativity, cognitive playfulness (Tan & McWilliam 2009), empathy and shared imagination. The open, metaphoric, project-based way of working in playbuilding shares much of what Daniel Pink (2005) refers to as the six essential attributes for success and satisfaction in the 21st-century: design, story, symphony, empathy, play and meaning. The wider field of education has much to gain from understanding the pedagogies of the drama classroom, where we work daily with students personal learning and meaning making as agentive and active creators.

Works cited

ACARA see Australian Curriculum, Assessment and Reporting Authority
Arnold R (1998). The drama in research and articulating dynamics: a unique theatre. In J Saxton & C Miller (Eds), *Drama and theatre in education: the research of practice: the practice of research*. Victoria, Canada: IDEA Publications.

Arnold R (2000). *Educating for empathic intelligence*. Faculty of Education, University of Melbourne, August [Online]. http://www.edfac.unimelb.edu.au/LLAE/new/Lecture.html [Accessed 18 August 2001].

Australian Curriculum, Assessment and reporting authority (2013) *Revised draft curriculum: the arts, Foundation to Year 10*. Sydney: Australian Curriculum, Assessment and Reporting Authority.

Barab S, Gresalfi M & Arici A (2009). Why educators should care about games. *Educational Leadership*, 67(1): 76–80.

Brook P (1993). *There are no secrets: thoughts on acting and theatre*. London: Methuen Drama.

Burton B (1991). *The act of learning*. Melbourne: Longman Cheshire.

Cope B & Kalantzis M (2009). Multiliteracies: new literacies, new learning. *Pedagogies: An International Journal*, 4(3): 164–95.

Davis S (2010). Creativity in drama: explanations and explorations. *NJ Drama Australia Journal*, 33(2): 32–43.

Dunn J (1996). Spontaneous dramatic play and the 'super-dramatist': who's structuring the elements of dramatic form? *NADIE Journal*, 20(2): 19–28.

Gee JP & Levine MH (2009). Welcome to our virtual worlds. *Educational Leadership*, 66(6): 49–52.

Greene M (1995). *Releasing the imagination: essays on education, the arts, and social change*. San Francisco: Jossey-Bass Publishers.

Haseman B & O'Toole J (1986). *Dramawise: an introduction to the elements of drama*. Richmond, Vic.: Heinemann Educational.

Hatton C (2005). Backyards and borderlands: transforming girls' learning through drama. PhD thesis, Sydney: University of Sydney.

Hatton C & Lovesy S (2009). *Young at art: classroom playbuilding in practice*. London: Routledge.

Heppell S (2012). Child led learning. Learning Without Frontiers Conference, London, January [Online]. Available: http://www.youtube.com/watch?v=_hrvli_wCT0 [Accessed 5 May 2013].

Kalantzis M, Cope B & the Learning by Design Group (2005). *Learning by design*. Melbourne: Victorian Schools Innovation Commission.

Linds W (1998). A journey in metaxis: theatre of the oppressed as enactivist praxis. *NADIE Journal*, 22(2): 71–85.

Lovesy S (2004). Secondary school playbuilding. PhD thesis, University of Western Sydney: Sydney.

McWilliam E (2008). Unlearning how to teach. *Innovations in Education and Teaching International*, 45(3): 263–69.

Moore C-L, & Yamamoto K (1988). *Beyond words: movement observation and analysis: instructor's guide*. New York: Gordon and Breach.

New London Group (1996). A pedagogy of multiliteracies: designing social futures. *Harvard Educational Review*, 66(1): 60 – 92.

O'Toole J (1992). *The process of drama: negotiating art and meaning*. London: Routledge.

O'Toole J (2002). Drama, the productive pedagogy. *Melbourne Studies in Education*, 43(2): 39–52.

Pink D (2005). *A whole new mind*. New York: Penguin.

Prensky M (2006). Listen to the natives. *Educational Leadership*, 63(4): 8–13.

Robinson K (2011). Creativity, learning and the curriculum. Learning Without Frontiers Conference, London, March [Online]. Available: http://www.youtube.com/watch?v=9X0CESnGQ8U&feature=player_embedded [Accessed 5 May 2013]

Schechner R (2002). *Performance studies: an introduction*. London: Routledge.

Smith D & Lovat TJ (1991). *Curriculum action on reflection*. Rev. edn. Sydney: Social Science Press.

Spolin V (1963). *Improvisation for the theatre*. Illinois: Northwestern University Press.

Tan J & McWilliam E (2009). Cognitive playfulness, creative capacity and generation 'C' learners. *Cultural Science*, 1(2): 1–7.

Turner VW (1982). *From ritual to theatre: the human seriousness of play*. New York: PAJ Publications.

Wagner BJ (1995). A theoretical framework for improvisational drama. *NADIE Journal*, 19(2): 61–70.

Wagner T (2008). *The global achievement gap: why even our best schools don't teach the new survival skills our children need – and what we can do about it*. New York: Basic Books.

Winnicott DW (1971). *Playing and reality*. London: Brunner-Routledge.

Winston J (2010). *Beauty and education*. London: Routledge.

5
Learning English as an additional language (EAL) through the pedagogy of educational drama

Margery Hertzberg

> When you have to use your imagination [in drama], you can think up better ideas ... so when you think, you must be learning English. (10-year-old EAL student)

The comment from this student is representative of what many EAL students from low socio-economic status backgrounds (SES) believe about the usefulness of drama for English learning and comes from data collected for the Fair Go Project (FGP). This article illustrates findings from the FGP and demonstrates why educational drama pedagogy as an art form is well placed for enhancing academic English, and at the same time, engenders EAL students from low SES backgrounds with a sense of engagement in the learning process and school in general. The term 'educational drama' is used to encapsulate the centrality of enactment within this pedagogical approach. As well, participants both lead and control the process with, when required, teacher/facilitator guidance. From here on however, the term 'drama' is used.

Hertzberg M (2015). Learning English as an additional language (EAL) through the pedagogy of educational drama. In M Anderson & C Roche (Eds). *The state of the art: teaching drama in the 21st century,* (85–108). Sydney: Sydney University Press.

The Fair Go Project

The first phase (2001–2004) of the Fair Go Project (FGP) was a partnership between the NSW 'Priority Schools Funding Program' and the University of Western Sydney's 'Pedagogy in Practice Research Group'. Since then other projects have been conducted (Munns et al. 2013). The program is based on the premise that student engagement is a critical condition for improved academic outcomes. Thus the FGP team (initially comprised of 10 university lecturers) set out to develop a pedagogical framework for student engagement. The FGP defines engagement in learning as something more than 'compliance' or 'on task' behaviour and so examines what pedagogical approaches might engage students. This view stems from an enduring long-term belief that educational achievement is a realistic aspiration for students from socio-economic and educationally disadvantaged backgrounds.

This initial project tested the FGP's model of engagement using each of the university researcher's respective skills and expertise. Each university researcher co-researched with full-time classroom teacher/s. My expertise is centred in developing and implementing drama teaching and learning sequences to improve EAL students' English.

Why drama for learning English as an additional language?

To be competent in conversational English takes about one to three years. To learn academic English (the language specific to a particular subject/content area) takes approximately seven to 10 years (Cummins 2008; Hakuta et al. 2000). Attaining academic English proficiency requires practice in a range of registers and language functions and is best achieved in authentic and believable situations (Cummins 2000; Gibbons 2009). Nevertheless, creating such situations is difficult because often the best situations to practise so many language forms may not be part of a school's regular program. This is why drama is well placed for language learning in the classroom. In drama, 'here and now' albeit fictional contexts are created to parallel reality. Through the process of enactment, students practise language across a range of situations (field) and through the status or relationship between the participants/actors (tenor) – hence the way the message is transmitted (mode) can be many and varied (Hertzberg 2012; Kao & O'Neill 1998; Liu 2002; Stinson 2008; Wagner 1998).

The drama pedagogy explained in this article emanates from dramatic play used by young children. Dramatic play enables the very young to create 'here and now' fictional contexts to enact stories. Through enactment they learn and practise a range of vocabulary and language structures in addition to the daily language of 'real life' home routine (Bruner 1986). Children play, for example, doctors and nurses/ going on a picnic/performing at a circus/cooking a pizza and so forth, to use language relevant to the situation. Furthermore, when adults join in the play they extend the talk by having conversations which usually involve open-ended questions and/or elaborated comments to further extend the scenario taking place (Arthur et al. 2012; Dockett & Fleer 2003; Hertzberg 2012). In so doing, adults importantly model new vocabulary and language structures to both enhance the drama and provide new language learning opportunities (Bruner 1993; Halliday 1985). But talking to practise vocabulary and grammar is not the only important reason.

Interacting with others is essential for abstract thinking and problem solving. In Vygotsky & Kozulin (1986), Vygotsky (1986) referred to this interactive talk with others as 'outer speech' maintaining that it allows us to think in different and imaginative ways as we negotiate with people. This in turn helps clarify concepts with ourselves, which Vygotsky termed 'inner talk' or 'verbal thought' to explain this abstract self-clarifying and/or problem-solving talk. As for young children, when older students are engaged in the process of enactment they are in authentic and hence believable (albeit fictional) situations to practise English for different purposes. Barrs et al. (2012) explain this using the term 'oral rehearsal' and elsewhere I have coined the term 'role to speak' (Hertzberg 2004a, 2012).

For the above reasons therefore, and not surprisingly, drama is a suggested task in all the worldwide EAL curriculum and supporting documents I have cited. Just one example for instance is the Western Australian EAL/D progress map, which informs some of the Australian Curriculum's teacher resource material (www.acara.edu.au). Either role play or other drama forms are suggested 29 times whereas completing a cloze task (for reading comprehension) is mentioned seven times. A similar statistic is true for all other documents cited. This is not to dismiss the extremely important benefits of the cloze strategy for language learning. Indeed, from anecdotal experience I suspect many teachers plan cloze tasks for students more frequently than drama tasks. The reasons for this may be varied but interrelated. Many specialist EAL teachers and mainstream teachers of EAL/D students have minimal or no drama training. For many untrained but 'willing to give it a go' teachers, initial attempts may not be successful and so understandably drama is relegated to the 'too hard basket', for as one of my co-researchers stated:

> I know that drama is a great way to get kids speaking and I do use puppetry quite a bit for that reason, but I find role-plays a real problem because [it] always ends up ... [a bit of mess].

However, this teacher began to use drama regularly after the results from this research indicated that drama both improved English learning and engaged students.

The Fair Go Project's pedagogical framework for student engagement

The project was influenced and informed by the research of both 'authentic' pedagogy (Newmann & Associates 1996) and 'productive pedagogies', (QSRLS 2001) as well as Bernstein's (1996) important research about how the type of curriculum planning can convey messages to students that influence their attitude to learning. The notion of engagement became the central focus of the FGP, based on the premise that student engagement is a critical condition for improved academic outcomes. In most of the research schools (all in south-western Sydney) there were a high percentage of EAL learners (in some schools as high as 98 percent) and these learners were from a diversity of backgrounds and experiences, including Indigenous students and students from refugee family backgrounds (FGPT 2006).

There is always the risk of stereotyping, but data from teacher interviews confirmed that many low SES students found engaging with school, and by implication learning, problematic (FGPT 2006; Munns 2007; Munns et al. 2013). Many teachers had high academic expectations for their students, but many students resisted the challenge because they did not sense that academic achievement was their prerogative – it was seen as the domain for advantaged groups, but not part of their reality. At times a vicious circle ensued with students resisting more challenging work but willing to participate in low challenging procedural tasks, and so a sense of compliance set in. With few exceptions, classrooms were peaceful places, but for many were students learning below their full potential. This is why the FGP centralises student engagement as the driving force to enhance both learning and social outcomes, so that students will 'buy into' the educational experience and hence have a long-term belief that educational achievement *is* a realistic aspiration for them.

The FGP's definition of engagement

The FGP uses the term 'in task' as opposed to 'on task' when determining engagement, because the word 'in' suggests more of a commitment—that one is inside the metaphorical space. Conversely, the word 'on' suggests being on the borderline and/or surface level of the metaphorical space. Thus the FGP maintains that students completing low level, low challenging tasks are not really committed to learning and are not 'in task'; rather they are being compliant. Further, the FGP identifies two forms of engagement: small 'e' engagement and big 'E' engagement. Small 'e' engagement is when students are involved in open-ended substantive learning tasks (in task). Because the FGP views engagement as a feeling or an emotion that is internalised, the FGP asserts that when students experience appropriate pedagogy over extended and sustained periods of time (usually longer than a year), big 'E' engagement might be achieved because students have developed a personal commitment and trust in themselves. That is, the students might have a long-term belief that 'school is for me' and so the FGP team uses the term 'future in the present' based on the notion that the future (school is for me) is within the present (in task 'e'ngagement), as illustrated in Figure 5.1.

The FGP contends that pedagogical processes that achieve small 'e' engagement are 'high cognitive' (a task that requires deep thinking and by implication problem solving), 'high affective' (a task that promotes

The state of the art

Figure 5.1 Links between 'e' and 'E' – 'the future in the present'

committed feelings while doing) and 'high operative' (actively involved in the doing). In classes where this process is occurring there appears to be an inextricable link between all three (Hertzberg et al. 2006; Munns et al. 2012; Munns et al. 2013), as seen in Figure 5.2.

The outer circle of this same figure (Figure 5.2) describes what the FGP refers to as 'insider' classroom processes. These processes are inextricably linked to and support the learning experiences, because students view themselves as an important part of a reflective learning community driven by teacher inclusive conversations, student self-assessment, and teacher feedback. Within this reflective learning community teachers send messages that both validate and respect the role of the student in the pedagogical process. Therefore, and in tandem with the engagement framework in Figure 5.2 above, Table 5.1 below illustrates the five messages identified by the FGP as 'engaging messages' for low SES students. The FGP contends that when students receive positive messages about their knowledge, their ability, their role in classroom control, their place and their voice they have a feeling of empowerment and are able to enact the term 'discourses of power'.

5 Learning English as an additional language

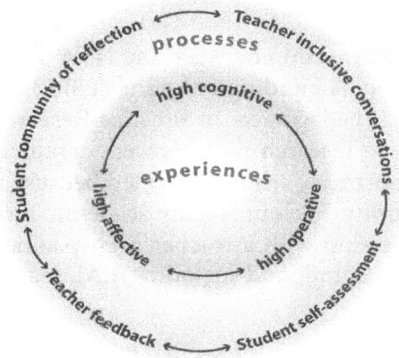

Figure 5.2 The Fair Go Project engagement framework – small 'e' engagement

Table 5.1 Discourses of power and engaging messages for low SES Students

Aspect	Message
knowledge	'We can see the connection and the meaning' – reflectively constructed access to contextualised and powerful knowledge
ability	'I am capable' – feelings of being able to achieve and a spiral of high expectations and aspirations
control	'We do this together' – sharing of classroom time and space: interdependence, mutuality and power
place	'It's great to be a kid from . . .' – valued as individual and learner and feelings of belonging and ownership over learning
voice	'We share' – environment of discussion and reflection about learning with students and teachers playing reciprocal meaningful roles

This FGP model of engagement was used in the research described below.

Research context

The project was a partnership between the NSW Department of Education's 'Priority Schools Funding Program' (PSFP) and the University of Western Sydney's 'Pedagogical in Practice Research Group'. Over a three-year period ten research projects were conducted in nine PSFP south-west Sydney primary schools, selected because of the low SES of the student community. Each university academic formed a collaborative research partnership with a teacher/s, co-planned and co-taught. With all students in mind, and including EAL learners, my research questions were:

1. Is educational drama a pedagogy that might provide engaging messages for low SES students?
2. Is educational drama a pedagogy that might enhance language and literacy outcomes and if so what factors might make this so?

In line with socio-cultural linguistic approaches (e.g. Cummins 2000; Gibbons 2009), the lesson sequences to research these questions placed an emphasis on using drama to promote oracy prior to and during reading and writing tasks.

This article refers to two sites and the teachers did not have drama training. The research was primarily undertaken in Site A, a mainstream 5/6 class (10, 11 and 12-year-olds) at a primary school in the Liverpool area. The co-researchers were the mainstream class teacher Kerrie Foord and EAL teacher Melissa Magna. I co-taught for 1½ hours each fortnight over one school year. The students were from cultural and linguistically diverse low SES backgrounds and 62 percent of students needed EAL assistance. As most had been learning English for at least five years their conversational English was good, but their academic English required attention. Further, it could be argued that most students needed extra English support irrespective of language background. Site B was a primary school in a housing estate near Campbelltown and my co-researcher Susan Barrett taught Year 5 (10 and 11-years-old). I co-researched with Susan for two hours per fortnight over ten weeks. The cohort was similarly culturally and linguistically diverse but with a higher proportion of Indigenous students.

We used ethnographic methodology, with a combination of case study and action research. Data were collected through observation and discussion between the university-based researcher and the classroom teacher-based researcher, and from student written work samples, video, photos, field notes, semi-structured interviews and focus groups with students and staff.

Analysing data

Student and teacher interviews, researchers' field notes, student work samples and photos were analysed and then coded based on emergent themes identified in the Fair Go Project model of student engagement. Specifically data were coded according to whether they demonstrated that the task was high cognitive and/or high affective and/or high operative for a specific student and/or small group of students and/or whole class. These same data were also analysed and coded for evidence that the drama pedagogy provided students with engaging messages as defined in the FGP's 'Discourses of power and engaging messages for low SES students' (knowledge, ability, control, place and voice). To analyse how and why this drama pedagogy assisted English learning, data were analysed according to the socio-cultural linguistic principles of English language learning.[1]

Reporting findings

Space precludes reporting all findings so just two drama teaching and learning sequences are analysed from Site A. When discussing engagement more generally, findings from both Site A and B are reported. Priority is given to both student work samples and opinions from interview data, following the premise that for many students from low SES backgrounds to be capable of long-term engagement, they first need to feel confident that school can be 'for them'. Their voices need to be heard and analysed. The findings illustrate that this drama pedagogy

---

1   Data were also coded to examine if the drama/English plans fulfilled the requirements of the NSW Department of Education and Training's 'Quality Teaching Model' (2003). This is not discussed in this article but readers are referred to Hertzberg 2004b.

engaged many previously disengaged students. This is exemplified by the comment of one of the most disaffected students I have ever taught. In interview he told me 'he loved drama'. Playing devil's advocate I suggested he might like drama because it wasted time from what he might regard as 'real work', but he vehemently stated that:

> It's (drama) NOT wasting time because wasting time means like you're out of it, like you're not doing anything (and) you're just sitting there bored, but if you are in it, it's like it's fun and then you're learning. (Site B)

To demonstrate improved learning outcomes and improved commitment to learning, two snapshots from Site A follow to highlight how incorporating drama within an English program adds a level of deep understanding. First, each learning sequence is summarised, with a discussion for each in terms of the FGP model of engagement and the socio-cultural linguistic principles of English learning. Second, both sequences are discussed more generally in terms of the engaging messages received (discourses of power).

Learning sequence 1. Sculpting a prominent issue/theme in a narrative to enhance interpretative comprehension and acquire new vocabulary

The aim was to analyse critically the theme of bullying in a picture book (Geoghegan & Moseng 1993) in preparation for reading it with the students' younger buddy class. While the written text is simple (although challenging for some students), the theme of emotional abuse on the basis of difference was age appropriate as was the concept of anthropomorphism.

Lesson sequence

1. The anticipated outcomes from the departmental syllabus document and definitions of fable and anthropomorphism were displayed and explained.
2. Teacher read the book to students.

3. An excerpt of written text was displayed. It is about one pig (Paprika) being ridiculed by five other pigs for being different – having a straight tail.
4. Students wrote a response to the following question: How do you think Paprika felt and why?
5. Working in pairs, one student sculpted the other as Paprika to show his/her interpretation of this scene.
6. Class viewed and discussed the different interpretations and then brainstormed appropriate vocabulary to describe these sculptures (Paprika).
7. Students returned to their previous written response to add additional information

Discussion and implications in terms of English language learning

Opportunity for a more in-depth and elaborate written response

Students were asked to write their response before doing the drama activity, because we wanted to find out if they had more to write after the sculpting exercise. Most did. Josie's example follows:

(Before sculpting she wrote)
Paprika must have felt like being the other person instead of the bullied one. She also must of felt alone.

(After sculpting she added)
She felt depressed and the other person is feeling guilty. She felt discriminated. When I did the activity I felt that I was Paprika and felt alone.

Josie's sample demonstrates the use of more descriptive vocabulary to express further ideas gleaned from this four-minute drama activity. Note also the affective response about feeling like Paprika. This response was not unique in the written samples and in interview students responded similarly. This result corresponds with Barrs et al. (2012), who state that in role:

> [students] are able to access other ways of talking ... Putting oneself in somebody else's shoes ... can enable someone to get closer to that person's thinking and way of using language ... [and] in the process they broaden their own linguistic range. (18)

In the EAL literature, the importance of interrupting the teacher initiates – student responds – teacher evaluates (IRE) cycle is important because it often limits both the amount and type of talking students produce, especially in a whole class situation (Cummins 2000; Gibbons 2009). Furthermore, the research of Mercer (2000) demonstrated that 'exploratory talk' as opposed to simple descriptive responses improves a student's ability to reason and problem solve.

As identified in teachers' field notes all students were involved actively in sustained 'exploratory talk' when discussing the concept to prepare their sculpture. The excerpt from one pair's talk demonstrates this:

> Put your head down and sit kind of squashed up so you look really lonely and close your eyes to show that you want to ignore them, but look really sad too because they are trying to discriminate against you and make you feel bad.

All students interviewed thought their 'oral rehearsals' (Barrs et al. 2012) gave them a 'role to speak' (Hertzberg 2004a & 2012), and subsequently helped them write their ideas. Ahmed's statement is representative:

> Like if you write it, you don't talk to anyone and you just think it out in your head ... you don't get to give your opinions [like you do in drama] and then you can use them [in your writing].

The above example of 'exploratory talk' reveals an oral comprehension exercise at an interpretative level.

5 Learning English as an additional language

Learning Sequence 2. Using questioning in role to enhance inferential comprehension

Issues around migration feature in the picture book *Marianthe's story* (Aliki 1998). With no country names disclosed, the story universalises themes such as displacement, language and custom barriers. Much of the story is only told in the visual text.

1. To connect students to just one major theme before reading the book, students were asked to prepare individual still images to convey how they might feel going to a new school unable to speak English.
2. Students brainstormed for vocabulary to convey this feeling and used these words later in a voice collage.
3. Teacher read the book.
4. Students reread the book in pairs (there were enough copies for one book per pair).
5. The drama strategies of sculpting, voice collage, still image, role walk and parallel improvisation were then used to interpret the narrative's major and varied themes (refer to Hertzberg 2004b).
6. The drama strategy of Questioning in Role (Q in R) was used. The father is a central character, however the father's migration from a war-torn country to a prosperous safe country is not detailed. All we know is that he left before his wife and children to earn money and find suitable accommodation. He wrote a letter about this but the story does not reveal its contents. The father (teacher in role) was questioned to find out his location, circumstances and feelings. Using this information, students in pairs wrote the father's letter to his family.

Discussion and implications in terms of English learning

Opportunity for a more in-depth and elaborate written response

One of the most compelling qualities of picture books is that they leave 'spaces to play', a term first coined by Williams (1991). The illustration of Uncle Theo reading the father's letter without supporting written text leaves such a 'space' and Q in R enabled students to infer about the father's probable experiences. Students found Q in R before writing helpful, for as one student stated, 'I'll be able to use this during the [national] writing test'. When asked to explain she elaborated:

> Well if I pretend that I'm doing drama [Q in R] then I'll use my imagination and come up with some good ideas, because they [writers of the test] give you a picture [and you have to use this to write a story] and I never know what to write about.

Many questions to begin the Q in R were mundane and/or closed, but students soon realised (without prompting from teachers) that open-ended analytical questions were needed to enable a substantive story to unfold. One teacher took notes as the story progressed and this summary was then printed and distributed to each pair to use as the 'back bone' for their letter. The letter below (corrected only for spelling, punctuation and grammar) was not the best example. It was selected for this article because it was written by two students performing well below age and grade expectations. Their commitment to school and learning was negative. Yet their teachers said it was their best work to date. Their letter is in accord with Booth and Neelands' research (1998) about using drama to improve writing. They contend that:

> The experience of taking on a character in drama also provided many students with enhanced empathy and understanding for a broad range of people . . . [allowing] them to write sensitively and genuinely from a variety of different points of view . . . Finding out about a character by asking questions and listening to and watching the responses the character makes . . . will flesh out literally, the student's own ideas. (pp20–22)

For many in this cohort, migration is part of their schematic knowledge and the EAL literature (e.g. Cummins et al. 2006) highlights the importance of connecting with students' schematic knowledge as a means of extending learning. This was one reason for selecting this book. In addition, the data indicate that Q in R helped students use their 'text analyst practices' (Freebody 2004) to read critically inferred meanings with an extra dimension of sensitivity and awareness. Both these as-

5 Learning English as an additional language

pects may have contributed to these boys exceeding expectations. As one said:

> My Dad's a refugee and he always tells me how lucky I am and how great Australia is and like I sort of understand, but now I reckon I understand deeper because I had to really think about it [the issues] to do the drama.

3/16 Stacey St
Liverpool NSW 2170
Australia

16th August 2003

My dear wife and children,
Thank you soooooooooooooooooooo much for the letters. Mari your writing is really good. Do you like going to school? I really miss you all, but I'm Okay. I have moved to a new flat in Liverpool which is good because it is closer to the factory that I work at. I have made friends with the people next door. They have twins, but they are girls and not boys. They are cute and remind me of the boys. The mother's name is Rima and she cooks nice food and I play cards with her husband.
Well I have to go now because I am tired.
I can't wait until I have enough money so you can come here.
Lots of love
    Dad
    xxxxxxxxxxxxxxoooooooooooooooooooooooooxxxxxxxxxx

PS Mari the kids are nice here and will be kind to you at school.

Bolton (1992) explains that drama provides a pivotal learning opportunity because of the link between the fictional world and reality. He terms this 'metaxis' (seeing two worlds at the same time). For this student, an in-depth examination of this narrative provided such an opportunity as he re-examined his own life and circumstances. Not only was his writing superior to previous attempts, he was affectively 'e'ngaged.

Discussion and implications in terms of 'e'ngagement

Teacher's field notes consistently noted that during drama most students appeared to be 'in task' as opposed to compliantly 'on task', or not compliantly 'off task' (as was often the case with the authors of the letter just examined). Making a comment about the cohort generally, Melissa wrote:

> Students are on task and excited about doing the activities requested ... even the shy students are giving it a go. There is no apprehension or avoidance behaviour on their part.

That most students were 'in' task during both the above sequences is now analysed in terms of the FGP's model of student engagement. Data from student interviews and work samples indicate that the sequences were high cognitive, high operative and high affective as detailed in Table 5.2.

Table 5.2 Data as matched with FGP's engagement framework – small 'e' engagement

---

High cognitive (students are thinking hard in challenging intellectual experiences)

Students were required to 'put themselves in someone else's shoes' and have sustained exploratory talk with their partner about the issues in order to interpret the theme. This is confirmed by a student who stated that:

> when I talk about it [bullying] during drama I can think of heaps better ways of saying and I have more to say.

Another student said that he had:

> to think more and I knew more about Bill. I had more ideas but my friend helps me write it because I can't write good.

High operative and high affective (students are actively involved in open-ended tasks which stimulate them with a sense of enjoyment)

It was difficult to differentiate between 'doing' and 'feeling' in order to code them as discrete results. This association might well indicate that being actively involved gives more commitment to one's beliefs/feelings as demonstrated in the following comment:

---

5 Learning English as an additional language

> 'It's fun to do it and not just do the writing . . . because you're doing it!' (Site A)

The word 'feel' was used time and again in interviews. Students commonly made comments such as:

> because you're actually being the person you have to work it out and see how it feels.

Such statements might suggest that the fictional context enables students through enactment to connect with different viewpoints, or as one student put it:

> 'Like isn't that the whole idea for doing drama because even though you're not really doing it because it's pretend you can feel what other people are feeling and learn more.' (Site A)

However, a lesson's content cannot be seen in isolation to the messages that such open-ended activities provide in terms of student empowerment in the learning process. They work in tandem (Munns et al. 2012; Munns et al. 2013).

Discussion and implications in terms of 'Discourses of power and engaging messages for low SES students'

When analysing student interview data and coding it to the 'Discourses of power and engaging messages for low SES students' framework, the importance for frequently using drama for English learning becomes even more compelling as demonstrated in Table 5.3. Data are used from both Site A and B.

Table 5.3 Data as matched with the FGP's 'Discourses of power and engaging messages for low SES students'

> **Knowledge** ('We can see the connection and the meaning' – reflectively constructed access to contextualised and powerful knowledge)

> Providing intellectually demanding work that students deem relevant is one of the most challenging aspects when working with disengaged low SES students. As discussed previously, for many students entering a fictional world can provide a schematic connection and this seems to create a depth of enthusiasm for learning for as one student stated:

If you're acting you can be a little more passionate about it. Acting gives you more of a picture of what you're actually doing instead of just writing it. When you write it, it doesn't stay for long, but if you act it, it's a memory. (Site A)

Ability ('I am capable' – feelings of being able to achieve and a spiral of high expectations and aspirations)

The comments below are representative of many students. They indicate feelings of being able to achieve, and the FGP maintains that if this attitude remains consistent over time students might well continue to have high expectations and aspirations.

I like it [drama] because I can think big ideas and plus I'm allowed to share them with my friends and I like how we work in groups and have to think for ourselves and I think Miss likes it because we are all good and we work heaps more and then she is happy. (Site B)

I love drama because I love acting and telling my story that way. (Site B)

Control ('We do this together' – sharing of classroom time and space: interdependence, mutuality and power with)

I really like doing reading this way. At first I was nervous because the teacher wants me have my own opinions. (Site A)

This comment indicates the sharing of classroom time and space. However, having opinions and sharing with others when not confident about one's ability involves risk taking. This may be why many low SES students feel safer working on low level procedural tasks as opposed to open-ended problem solving tasks. But enactment can provide a safe haven, for as one student said:

I like drama, 'cause you can say things that are you, but nobody has to know because you are acting someone else. (Site A)

Risk taking was, according to some students, aided by working in friendship groups.

[I like working with friends] because you like them and they like you and then it's easier ... you don't worry about them laughing and all that, so you say more (Site A).

Place ('It's great to be a kid from ...' – valued as individual and learner and feelings of belonging and ownership over learning

Possibly this message is the most problematic and difficult to achieve and yet perhaps crucial, especially for those showing considerable oppositional behaviour. Many students see education as a middle-class prerogative and not available to them. Being valued as a learner and having feelings of belonging and ownership over learning can 'turn these kids around' as evidenced from one such student.

> [Drama is] better, funner, teaching more than doing unjumble the sentence. I just do one of them [unjumble the sentence] and then sit there pretending to do more but I don't. It's [drama] teaching more and having fun. (Site B)

Voice ('We share' – environment of discussion and reflection about learning with students)

In the 'drama circle' reflective dialogue which followed many activities, one student said that he thought the way the lessons were sequenced (scaffolded although he did not use this term) was important:

> because the teacher gives you the bones of it and we have to act the muscles. (Site A)

Whilst the teacher initiated the task, the children must take ownership and by implication take the risk to provide the substance. Further, the drama circle provided an environment of discussion and reflection about learning where students and teachers played reciprocal roles, as exemplified by the student who said:

> Well I didn't like it [drama circle], because you [teacher] didn't make [many] comments so I never knew if I was right or wrong, but now I do [like it] because I've got used to it and I just say what I think and it's fun when other people join in. (Site B)

Limitations

First, as a small-scale piece of qualitative research, there is insufficient longitudinal data. Notwithstanding this, the study does contribute to the body of research that examines the benefits of this drama pedagogy for language and literacy development.

Second, in many books and articles where students' perceptions about drama are discussed, there are at times qualifications of modality with words such as 'most students . . .' or 'for many students . . .'. This word choice acknowledges that not all students like drama and hence may not be 'e'ngaged. This might apply to this cohort. However, no negative data was collected from either site even though in interview I probed with questions such as 'well I'm pleased you enjoyed the drama (name of student) but maybe there are other ways that you would prefer to learn' or 'it's good that you thought it was fun, but maybe you were not learning anything?' Possibly an interviewer detached from the teaching may have got some negativity due to anonymity. This is an important consideration for future research. Data from teacher interviews and field notes indicated that teachers saw significant improvements in English for many individual students, as well as improved attitudes to school from the cohort as a whole. However, some students may have felt duty-bound to say what they thought the teacher wanted to hear and not mention aspects they did not like and/or did not find useful for learning. We suspect the rebellious students did express their true opinions as there was no hesitation to make negative statements about other areas of their school experience; nevertheless this an issue for future consideration with well-behaved compliant students.

Conclusion

That drama assists EAL students is well known by EAL theorists and policymakers, which is why almost all EAL curriculum and supporting documents worldwide program for the regular use of drama. Drama provides students with 'a role to speak' in authentic situations and this 'oral rehearsal' aids students' 'inner thinking/speech' which in turn assists both their reading and writing. But that drama can engage disengaged students with learning may not be as well known. This research demonstrated that for these low SES students, the regular inclusion of drama may over time contribute to an enduring long-term belief that education is an achievable aspiration for them and not just for students from advantaged backgrounds.

However, EAL teachers with minimal training in drama do not know why the features unique to drama make it so effective for language learning. As drama educators we must make clear to our non-specialist colleagues the power of drama and I suggest the following three interrelated reasons for a good beginning.

The first is the power of *enactment*. When the content to be examined is both age appropriate and academically challenging, role-taking for many students enables risk-taking because the enactment process protects them from either making a mistake as their 'real self' or revealing their 'real self' opinions. For many students this safety net within enactment often leads to profound and committed feelings about the issues and frequently promotes sustained, considered and in-depth analytical conversations. Furthermore, enactment enables students to interpret or infer information in both factual and fictional texts from different points of view. Assessing how another person's perspective positions oneself is a central tenet of critical literacy.

Second, the pedagogical approach to studying *subject content* in drama is significant. While the teacher often (but not always) determines the subject area and supporting resources, the ideas and materials for the drama are always negotiated and developed *with* students. This provides students with a commitment to their ideas and ownership over their learning as evidenced, for instance, when studying *Marianthe's story*.

Third, the concept of metaxis (being able to see the world of fiction and the world of reality at the same time), enables students to make authentic and purposeful connections. The ideas/themes/issues are contextualised within the fictional setting but importantly they are then transferrable to the real world. This helps many students better understand and empathise with big ideas and concepts in other areas. To make this connection the significance of the reflection process during the drama is central. The substantive conversations with and between students about their drama not only aid in making immediate connections but many times extend the process leading to enhanced examination of the content and thus further English learning opportunities.

Nevertheless, despite drama's benefits, there remains another perceived stumbling block to using drama. Many teachers feel pressured by time constraints. Incorporating drama into English programs does make the program longer. However, as demonstrated previously, students believed the extra time taken to incorporate drama before and during reading and writing was helpful. The time factor was raised with Melissa when we discussed whether her program aims could have been achieved more quickly or efficiently without drama.

> No. No way. I don't think so. Yes, it's much longer than giving a very expository lesson and saying 'OK, we've read this passage and now I want you to go away and write your opinion about Jack and why you think he finds it difficult to talk to his Mum'. Or 'OK, now let's look at how the author has used direct and indirect speech' and then have a

teacher-directed question time. But drama – OK, it did take longer – but all the kids are involved and I really think they are learning more and more deeply, and that's for me what quality teaching is about. It's not how long or short the lesson is that matters – it's whether they are learning anything substantial. This comes back to the point I made about risk-taking earlier [in this interview]. I said many kids here don't like to take risks. They don't want to do anything wrong. They are so scared of getting it wrong. They would rather just do tick-and-flick stencils, but drama takes them outside that box, out of that comfort zone, and they have to really think about the content, which leads to deeper understanding.

Works cited

Aliki (1998). *Marianthe's story: painted words, spoken memories.* New York: Greenwillow Books.

Arthur L, Beecher B, Death E, Dockett S & Farmer S (2012). *Programming and planning in early childhood settings.* 5th edn. Melbourne: Cengage.

Barrs M, Barton B & Booth D (2012). *This book is not about drama . . . it's about new ways to inspire students.* Markham, ON: Pembroke Publishers.

Bernstein B (1996). *Pedagogy, symbolic control and identity: theory, research, critique.* London: Taylor & Francis.

Bolton G (1992). *New perspectives on classroom drama.* London: Simon & Schuster Education.

Booth D & Neelands J (Eds) 1998. *Writing in role: classroom projects connecting writing and drama.* Hamilton, ON: Caliburn Enterprises.

Bruner J (1986). Play, thought and language. *Prospects: Quarterly Journal of Education,* 16: 76–83.

Bruner J (1993). *Actual minds, possible worlds.* Cambridge, MA: Harvard University Press.

Cummins J (2000). *Language, power and pedagogy.* Clevedon, UK: Multilingual Matters.

Cummins J (2008). BICS and CALP: empirical and theoretical status of the distinction. In B Street & N Hornberger (Eds). *Encyclopaedia of language and education* (pp71–83). 2nd edn. New York: Springer Science + Business Media.

Cummins J, Bismilla V, Chow P, Cohen S, Giampapa F, Leoni L et al. (2006). *ELL students speak for themselves: identity, texts and literacy engagement in multilingual classrooms* [Online]. Available: www.curriculum.org/secretariat/files/ELLidentityTexts.pdf [Accessed 13 August 2011].

5 Learning English as an additional language

Dockett S & Fleer M (2003). *Play and pedagogy in early childhood: bending the rules*. 2nd edn. Sydney: Harcourt Brace.

Fair Go Project Team (2006). *School is for me: pathways to student engagement*. Sydney: Priority Schools Programs, NSW Department of Education and Training.

Freebody P (2004). Hindsight and foresight: putting the four roles model of reading to work in the daily business of teaching. In A Healy & E Honan (Eds). *Text next: new resources for literacy learning* (pp3-17). Sydney: Primary English Teaching Association.

Gibbons P (2009). *English learners' academic literacy and thinking: learning in the challenge zone*. Portsmouth, NH: Heinemann.

Geoghegan A & Moseng E (1993). *Six perfectly different pigs*. London: Hazar.

Hakuta K, Butler Y & Witt D (2000). *How long does it take English learners to attain proficiency?* The University of California Linguistic Minority Research Institute Policy Report 2000-1 [Online]. Available: www.stanford.edu/~hakuta/www/research/publications.html 5_Acquiring-a-Second-Language-for-School_DLE4.pdf [Accessed 13 August 2011].

Halliday MAK (1985). *Spoken and written language*. Geelong: Deakin University Press.

Heathcote D & Bolton G (1995). *Drama for learning: Dorothy Heathcote's mantle of the expert approach to education*. Portsmouth, NH: Heinemann.

Hertzberg M (2004a). Unpacking the drama process as intellectually rigorous – 'The teacher gives you the bones of it and we have to act the muscles'. *NJ (Drama Australia Journal)*, 28(2): 41-53.

Hertzberg M (2004b). Drama when English is an additional language. In R Ewing & J Simons with M. Hertzberg. *Beyond the script. Take two: drama in the classroom* (pp93-108). Sydney: Primary English Teaching Association.

Hertzberg M, Foord K & Manga M (2006). Dramatically 'e'ngaged. In Fair Go Project Team, *School is for me: pathways to student engagement*. Sydney: Priority Schools Program, NSW Department of Education and Training.

Hertzberg M (2012). *Teaching English language learners in mainstream classes*. Sydney: Primary English Teaching Association.

Kao SM & O'Neill C (1998). *Words into worlds: learning a second language through process drama*. Stamford, CT: Ablex.

Liu J (2002). Process drama in second and foreign language classrooms. In G Brauer (Ed). *Body and language: intercultural learning through drama* (pp51-70). Westport: Greenwood.

Mercer N (2000). *Words and minds: how we use language to think together*. New York: Routledge.

Munns G (2007). A sense of wonder: pedagogies to engage students who live in poverty. *International Journal of Inclusive Education*, 11(3): 301–15.

Munns G, Arthur L, Hertzberg M, Sawyer W & Zammit K (2012). A fair go for students in poverty: Australia. In T Wrigley, R Thomson & R Lingard (Eds). *Changing schools: alternative ways to make a world of difference* (pp167–80). London: Routledge.

Munns G, Sawyer W & Cole B (Eds) (2013). *Exemplary teachers of students in poverty*. London: Routledge.

Newmann F & Associates (1996). *Authentic achievement: restructuring schools for intellectual quality*. San Francisco: Jossey Bass.

NSW Department of Education and Training: Professional Support and Curriculum Directorate (2003). *Quality teaching in NSW public schools, a classroom practice guide*. Sydney: NSW Department of Education and Training.

Queensland School Reform Longitudinal Study (QSRLS) (2001) submitted to Education Queensland by the School of Education, University of Queensland, State of Queensland (Department of Education), Brisbane.

Stinson M (2008). Drama, process drama, and TESOL. In M Anderson, J Hughes & J Manuel (Eds). *Drama in English teaching: imagination, action and engagement* (pp193–212). Oxford: Oxford University Press.

Wagner BJ (1998). *Educational drama and language arts: what research shows*. Portsmouth, NH: Heinemann.

Williams G (1991). Space to play: the use of analyses of narrative structure in classroom work with children's literature. In M Saxby & G Winch (Eds). *Give them wings* (pp355–368). 2nd edn. South Melbourne: Macmillan.

Vygotsky L & Kozulin A (1986). *Thought and language*. Cambridge, MA: MIT Press.

Western Australia Department of Education. *Curriculum resources*. http://www.curriculum.wa.edu.au/internet/Years_K10/Curriculum_Resources

6
What's wrong with the way we teach playwriting?

Paul Gardiner

> Well I did the NIDA playwright's course years ago – people used to give me a little bit of money to write a play and I wrote, and I worked in a TIE [Theatre in Education] community theatre company, and I would create plays professionally. But I still think I am a better marker than I am a teacher of scriptwriting, though I am quite happy with other aspects of my teaching, I do not think that I am a very good scriptwriting teacher in year twelve.
>
> Mr B, St Martha's

While writing for performance is a core aspect of drama education and drama in education, many teachers approach teaching playwriting with trepidation and ambivalence. Additionally, much of teacher training and high school coursework is focused on devising performance, playwriting is unfortunately an activity on the periphery. I wish to explore the factors that may be contributing to teacher apprehension and to challenge this peripheral status. For many teachers in my study, teaching playwriting was an activity for which they felt unprepared and, as a consequence, many found the experience unsatisfying and frustrating, and considered their efforts to be less than effective. My research sought

Gardiner P (2015). What's wrong with the way we teach playwriting? In M Anderson & C Roche (Eds). *The state of the art: teaching drama in the 21st century*, (109–128). Sydney: Sydney University Press.

to understand what it was about the teaching of playwriting that caused such a response from highly successful and experienced teachers.

In an attempt to understand the experience for both teachers and students, I studied the playwriting process in a number of NSW secondary schools. I explored the playwriting experience for students and teachers in order to better understand the teaching and learning that was occurring in the classroom. One of the emerging themes was an aversion to accessing or employing playwriting texts or theory to inform the teachers' pedagogy, as they considered them to be formulaic and restrictive. To begin my research, I examined the resources available to teachers.

The background literature

An initial survey of the literature on playwriting suggests that Aristotle's *Poetics* (1996) and its focus on plot and a linear narrative still appeared to dominate the pedagogical approach. As McKean (2007) reports, 'most of the [playwriting] literature organises discussions on finding the shape or form of composition around a linear structure of beginning, middle and end'. Many of the playwriting 'how to' books (Catron 2002; Egri 1960; Jensen 1997; Selden 1946; Smiley 2005) either write based on this assumption or structure their approach based on Aristotle's headings. Yet this predominance is not without its opponents. Castagno (1993) comments that 'the litany of playwriting texts unhappily persists in the Aristotelian mold'. Waters (2012, 2) reminds us of the need to be wary of Aristotle's potentially negative influence, suggesting 'this poster-boy of formal perfection has too often served as a cudgel to beat into shape all sorts of equally good but formally eccentric works'. Norden (2007) was concerned that strict adherence to an 'Aristotelian' model could produce a 'cookie cutter' mentality and an over reliance on Freytag's 'pyramid' (Freytag 1900), bringing 'the practice of playwriting perilously close to the acceptance of standard story formats' (2007, 646). Reflecting this response, and seeing little relevance to their own practice, many playwrights are abandoning Aristotle and what they consider a prescriptive approach to the writing of plays. As Fornes recounts when considering the Aristotelian form: 'I looked at it and started laughing because I thought: How ridiculous, that's not the

6 What's wrong with the way we teach playwriting?

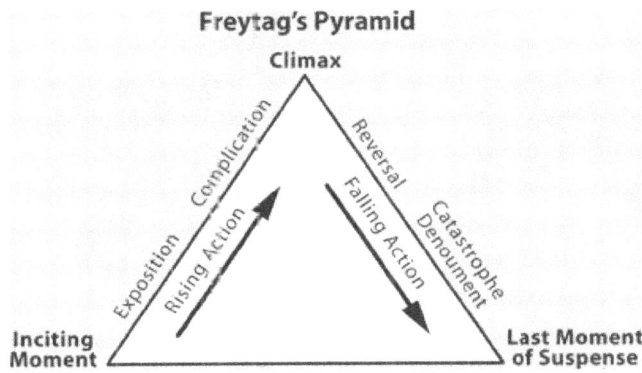

Figure 6.1 Freytag's Pyramid as a model for standard story format. (adapted from Freytag 1900, 114–140)

way life happens. And why should one try to follow a formula that has nothing to do with life? (cited in Herrington & Brian, 2006, 4).

But is this initial perception correct? Do the Aristotelian playwriting books represent the extent of resources available to the teacher and playwright? The short answer is 'no'.

A review of the broader literature on playwriting reveals that there is actually a spectrum of theoretical approaches available to the 'emerging' playwright and the teacher developing teaching and learning strategies to support the student in the process of writing a play. Roughly speaking, the end points of the spectrum can be described as 'closed' and 'open'.

The closed approach values plot resolution, centres on a single protagonist, struggling against both a fatal flaw and an opponent/antagonist. The approach can be said to reflect a worldview that assumes that 'certainty' is possible and that we are agents operating with free will. Plays of this ilk normally include resolved dilemmas, consistent characters, and 'witty and logically built up dialogue' (Esslin 1965). In many ways it assumes a tidiness of existence and presents a linear 'cause and effect' journey of character.

The open approach on the other hand is informed by the experience of 20th-century avant-garde theatre makers and reflects on an epistemological world view that I describe as 'embracing uncertainty

The state of the art

Figure 6.2 The theoretical spectrum of playwriting

without despair, and untidiness without chaos' and plays often choose not to resolve thematic ideas or demands of plot, and/or may adopt a cyclical structure that rejects a reliance on 'cause and effect'. They often include 'figure conceptions' rather than psychologically rounded characters. They do not assume the existence of an 'ultimate' meaning grounded in resolution and finality (Edgar 2009; Stephenson & Langridge 1997; Waxberg 1998).

The image of the spectrum is relevant, as it removes the idea of 'camps' of 'isms': realism, absurdism etc. It presents the conventions and techniques as a kind of theatrical smorgasbord. As a spectrum, each individual playwright may choose their own mix of open and closed aspects depending on the central idea and vision of the particular play they are writing. Despite Fornes' comment, this theatrical Machiavellianism doesn't privilege one approach over another – the worth of the approach is its ability to effectively communicate the playwrights' ideas and worldview – the ends must 'justify' the means.

This idea is clearly conveyed by Martin Esslin in his introduction to *Absurd drama* (1965). His explanation of the emergence of Absurdist theatre supports the view that forms, structures and conventions are tools; options not restrictions. Absurdist theatre, he argues, was born from the need to find a way to express each playwright's unique, revolutionary and 'personal view of the world' (14). Rather than creating new techniques, the undeniably transformative effect of these plays came from a 'new combination of a number of ancient, even archaic traditions' that were 'unusual and shocking merely because of the unusual nature of the combination and ... emphasis' (14). This view positions the playwright as being in control of the conventions and that knowledge of 'the rules' and of what came before, is an essential ingredient in this seismic shift in our definition of theatre. This view is echoed by Castagno and the New Language Playwrights, another group of writers re-inventing the form, who create text that 'appears strikingly new [but] in ways reformulates solid theatrical practices of the past' (Castagno, 2001).

Far from limiting creativity, the experience of the Theatre of the Absurd suggests that knowledge of styles, techniques and conventions are necessary for creating new approaches to form. Furthermore, this knowledge feeds the playwrights' theatrical semiotic 'vocabulary', enabling them to not only convey their existing ideas but opening them up to thoughts and ideas previously unfamiliar to them (Nicholson 1998). In this way, knowledge feeds creativity; developing a deep knowledge of the 'spectrum' could not only generate new forms, but also generate new ideas. As Waters (2012, 5) argues 'writing is always an intertextual act: the plays of our predecessors generate ones we've yet to dream up'. This would suggest that an effective pedagogical approach to playwriting should be informed by this spectrum. With knowledge of the literature available to the teachers in planning their pedagogy, I sought to research the impact of theory on classroom practice.

The study

This study sought to answer the question 'what are the teaching and learning experiences of students and teachers preparing a script for external assessment for the NSW Higher School Certificate Drama examination?'[2] It focused on and explored the teaching of the short play form – plays that are 15–25 pages in length and that occupy approximately 15 minutes stage time. For this research I used a comparative

---

2 The HSC course is studied over four terms and represents the final year of study in NSW schools. The course has three components: the written paper (40 percent), the group performance (30 percent) and the individual project (30 percent). For the individual project, students can choose from a range of areas, such as critical analysis, design, performance, scriptwriting and video drama, and the project is marked as a process internally in the school's assessment program and externally by HSC examiners.

case study approach studying five school sites and examined the Year 12 students writing a play for their individual project. As these particular drama classes had one student writing a play, the study focused on teacher–student pairs, therefore studying the experience of five teachers and five Year 12 student playwrights. For the purpose of anonymity, the participants are referred to using pseudonyms and the schools are indicated by fictitious acronyms.

The data was qualitative, collected using self-reporting instruments, such as semi-structured interviews and written reflections, and observations of process and product. The teachers and students were interviewed twice, once during and once after the process, with the second round picking up themes from the first. A playwriting mentoring session and play-reading workshop, where possible, were also observed for each school. The plays in draft and final form, as well as the students' reflective logbooks, were then collected as data for the study.

Emerging findings – the noble savage

Initially, the focus of the research was to investigate the impact of theoretical ideas in the teaching and learning activities on the students' plays. However, the emerging findings suggested participants, teachers and students, did not explicitly engage with the theory at all. While this lack of theoretical input was acknowledged by the teachers and students, it was often explained as a virtue not an omission. It reflects what I call the assumption of the 'noble savage' of playwriting and a distrust of 'teaching' or intervention. The image of the noble savage is particularly illuminating for understanding the teachers' belief that 'less is more' in playwriting pedagogy.

The noble savage is a 'mythic personification of natural goodness' (Ellingson 2001, 1), before the corrupting influence of civilisation, and represents a rich metaphor for this reluctance to engage in playwriting pedagogy. The concept posits that humanity is happier and morally superior in a 'state of nature', free from the sophistications of modern citizenship. Despite the fact this concept has a controversial place in anthropological discourse (see Ellingson 2001), Jackson (2001) argues that Rousseau (among others) contemplated the noble savage as a 'thought experiment' to suggest that ever since the 'Golden Age', humanity has been deteriorating. Rousseau's noble savage was a utopian symbol, a revolutionary ideal to combat absolutist rule and encourage republicanism (Greer 1993, 90). In the context of playwriting pedagogy, there are many interesting parallels. Fear of oppressive reliance on formula or the tainting of individuality by exposure to teaching reflects this belief that naive talent is 'noble' and should be kept free from the corrupting influence of theory. Waters (2012) calls this the 'myth of the natural playwright', one who 'doesn't need to read or think much about what they do because their plays ooze out of them effortlessly, like sweat from a pore' (6). This view reflects some teachers' understanding of creativity and the belief that creative tasks require minimal intervention to protect the students' natural voice. It refers to the teachers' views on what is possible or perhaps permissible education for a creative task.

On the issue of what constitutes appropriate pedagogy for a creative task, the literature and research reveal widespread tensions and ambivalence toward the value of teaching the craft. Playwrights and teachers alike express the view that teaching is counter-productive and diminishes the potential and uniqueness of the emerging playwright. Norden (2007) refers to playwrights' reluctance for writing to be 'taught' at all, quoting one writer who warned that 'creative writing courses damage a distinctive talent' (646). Herrington and Brian's (2006) question: 'Is there a danger that the very act of instruction can, in fact, stifle the creative promise?'(viii) suggests the view that teaching corrupts rather than edifies. Despite their employment in key tertiary education faculties, a number of American playwrights express reluctance to instruct students in the craft: Tony Kushner expresses a vehement disdain for academic teaching, arguing that 'no one needs to spend four years learning how to write a play. What you need to learn you learn by doing, and talent and application and luck take care of the rest of it' (Herrington & Brian 2006, 137). While he encourages extensive reading of plays and theory (144), the focus for learning the craft should be to 'write plays that are meant to be produced, rather than [writing] plays that satisfy assignments' (138). Maria Irena Fornes explains that one goes to workshops to write, not to talk or learn (15), and Rivera argues that, as a teacher, you can't improve or generate talent (Herrington and Brian 2006, viii). Mac Wellman suggests 'there are no rules' (Herrington & Brian 2006, 98) supporting Hwang's position that you are either a playwright or you are not (viii).

In practical terms teaching and learning, in the playwriting context, has been strongly influenced by the associated beliefs that the student, left to their own devices, will produce something 'authentic' and 'true', and that intervention will dilute their natural voice. And it is believed that the playwriting ability is a gift, something you are born with, that makes interventionist teaching seem redundant or damaging.

The teacher and the Muse

The fear that teaching limits, rather than develops a playwright, ignores the benefits of knowledge to creativity. It appears to have been influenced by a conception of creativity based upon a belief in the Muse, that the best teaching is to get out of the way to provide the opportunity for creativity to be released. As McIntyre (2012) suggests, despite creativity scholarship providing evidence that this popular view is perhaps not valid, respect for both the noble savage and the Muse still prevail.

In the playwriting teaching and learning I observed, there was very little teaching that explicitly covered the theoretical spectrum and, in fact, there was very little generic teaching at all. Most chose to, as one teacher indicated, 'get them writing so we have something to talk about' (Mr P from St Anne's). The teachers' views on their role suggest – at least at this point in the student's process – they believe in the noble savage approach. The teachers consider strategies that teach dialogue or character development would 'quash the student's original voice and stifle creativity' (Ms S from GLC). They all define themselves as facilitators and not instructors of playwriting, and see their role as predominantly 'editing and proofreading.' A number of teachers explained that the worth of this approach was its ability to nurture student creativity. One teacher, for example, proposes that in 'these projects, it's a kind of creative impulse that has to be just shaped and refined. I think that is my job: the shaping and refining in that editing process' (Ms S from GLC).[3] This process generally takes the form of 'negative

---

3   It must be noted that many teachers expressed their assumption that if students have chosen playwriting for the HSC they should already know how to do it. A number of the teachers had playwriting units in the Stage 5 program to give them the skills to write a play. While there is merit in that approach, many in the small

instruction',[4] where aspects of the play that didn't work are identified and ear-marked for improvement in the next draft.

In explaining the purpose of input, all but one of the teachers indicated they had no resources, only their 'understanding and experience of theatre' (Ms J from St Alexander's) which resides 'in their head' (Mr P from St Anne's), and that they 'garner the little bits that might be useful out of my encyclopedia of stuff [in my head]' (Ms S from GLC). The main approach is to direct students to read plays and produce drafts that the teacher would then annotate. This approach is specifically adopted because it is thought to be the best way to nurture the student's talent and to work 'organically' with their creative ideas. What was interesting about this approach was the absence of evidence that the students had read any plays during their preparation. Some had read none, and of those who had read plays only one went beyond the one or two examples given to them by the teacher.

Another significant theme that emerged was concerned student engagement with the process and with their play. A number of the students began with great enthusiasm, a desire to take risks and create challenging theatre. Many students clearly expressed their engagement with a process that was so creative it was 'unschool' (Phillipa from St Anne's) and a 'rejuverating distraction' from their other HSC work (Sam from St Alexander's); expressing enthusiasm for a task that gave them complete freedom and autonomy (Sarah from GLC). However, and perhaps surprisingly considering the rationale of their teachers' approach, the students became, to varying degrees, disengaged with the teacher and/or the project. At worst, some students became anxious, paralysed and/or blasé over the course of the process, with this disengagement leading to feelings of diminished ownership. Unfortunately, as engagement and ownership decreased, students became exam-results focused and were more likely to ask the teacher to '*now* tell me what to do to get the best mark'. Similarly, near the end of the process,

---

cohort involved in the study had chosen playwriting because they were not 'performers'. They were not keen playwrights and while they may have completed the earlier classwork, it became evident that they were not in possession of these skills.
4   This concept, coined by Samuel Selden in his *Introduction to playwriting* in 1946, has influenced playwriting pedagogy ever since.

the teachers were finding themselves providing more precise and prescriptive feedback to find solutions to the problems they had identified.

This tension, between the identified problems and the student paralysis, and between the impending deadline and the unfinished product, had a significant impact on the teacher–student dynamic. It raises the question of what teaching means in this context. It also questions the effectiveness of the noble savage assumptions in enabling the student to reach their potential. The research sought to examine the relationship, if any, between the noble savage approach and the students' inconsistent engagement. My research suggested that these themes may be connected and that there may even be a correlation between the 'negative instruction' (Selden 1946) approach and the observed decrease in engagement. As the rationale behind this approach is to respect the students' creativity, current thinking on creativity might shed some light on the experiences of these students and teachers. In particular, the systems' approach to creativity argues that there is a relationship between creativity, engagement, skill acquisition and knowledge.

Csikszentmihalyi and the flow channel

Csikszentmihalyi's systems theory of creativity, his concept of flow, and the conditions associated with its occurrence (Csikszentmihalyi 2008) provide evidence for the value of teaching and skill acquisition in creative tasks. As well as linking motivation and talent, and describing moments of extraordinary focus, 'flow' can also help us understand more common experiences of productive engagement.

Csikszentmihalyi explains that when the challenge of a particular task is met with a commensurate skill level the individual remains in the 'flow channel' (see Figure 6.3), a state of heightened awareness that is characterised by, among other things, a focus on a clear goal, a sense of control and a diminishing awareness of time passing. This experience is so enjoyable that the task becomes 'autotelic, that it is worth doing for its own sake (Csikszentmihalyi et al. 1993, 15) and encourages repetition (Csikszentmihalyi 1993, 39). Thus flow may be seen as the ultimate example of intrinsic motivation (Csikszentmihalyi 2008).
The key relationship is that to achieve flow and creativity we require an optimal match between skill and challenge. This is a dynamic process,

6 What's wrong with the way we teach playwriting?

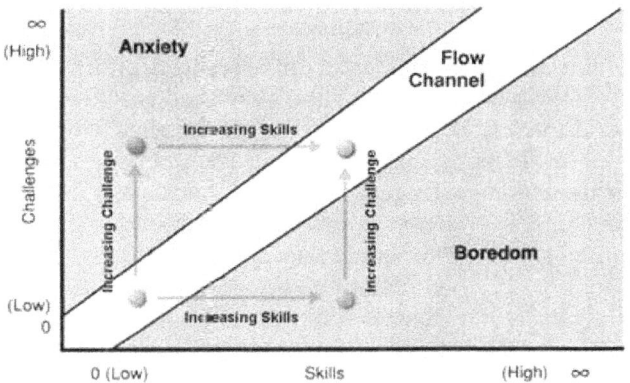

Figure 6.3 The Flow Channel (Adapted from Csikszentmihalyi 2008, 74)

that pushes people to higher levels of performance (Csikszentmihalyi 2008). As he explains further;

> Flow leads to complexity because, to keep enjoying an activity, a person needs to find ever new challenges in order to avoid boredom and to perfect new skills in order to avoid anxiety. The balance of challenges and skills is never static. (Csikszentmihalyi et al. 1993, 15)

This concept is particularly valuable for our understanding of self-directed learning for all students, not only those working on a play. For a student to engage – and then maintain that engagement – in a creative and challenging task, the skill level must continue to match the increasing challenge. This idea is reiterated by Starko who argues that 'if insufficient skill development precedes a challenging, potentially creative activity, it is likely to be met with frustration and resistance' (Starko 2005, 374). These last two concepts are key as they describe the experience of many of the students in my study who began with enthusiasm but lost focus, and became frustrated and resistant. They also exhibited paralysis and anxiety, responses found outside the flow channel. Perhaps an explanation is that the students 'fly up' out of the channel when the task presents a greater challenge than their skills can handle.

Students begin with an idea an initial kernel of creativity, that needs craft or aesthetic control to actualise. They need to know how to make their idea theatrical: how to manipulate the elements of drama to make it engaging, and how to create metaphor using theatre semiotics, with its signs and common language, to communicate to the audience. As Anderson suggests, our job as drama educators is to 'make the mysterious knowable, but more than knowable: it is to create a structured understanding of . . . aesthetics and to allow students to use that aesthetic to create their own work' (2012, 53). So how do we do that? What is the role of the teacher in enabling students? To answer that question, let's consider the focus of our efforts – the student.

The student playwright

In the interviews with teachers and students it is made clear that there are three distinct and interrelated aspects or components of the 'playwriting student', and that these work together to enable the student to write their play. Using these component parts I will explore what teachers can meaningfully and effectively do in this process of facilitation. In short, teaching should occur within the role of support to ensure that the student realises their true potential and that their creativity is nurtured with knowledge and empowered by skill.[5]

The first component is what I call the student's global understanding of theatre, developed from their experience of the performed and written script, and their knowledge and skills developed in the drama classroom. This is their ability to read and understand theatre and drama, and their ability to express that understanding. This is the most easily identified aspect, and is referred to by a number of the teachers in the study as being the foundation of any playwright. Specifically, from the teachers' perspective, this global view is established through

---

5 These component parts somewhat mirror the three sections of the marking guidelines for the scriptwriting individual project devised by the Board of Studies and applied to the plays submitted by the student. I would like to think that that is not coincidental.

6 What's wrong with the way we teach playwriting?

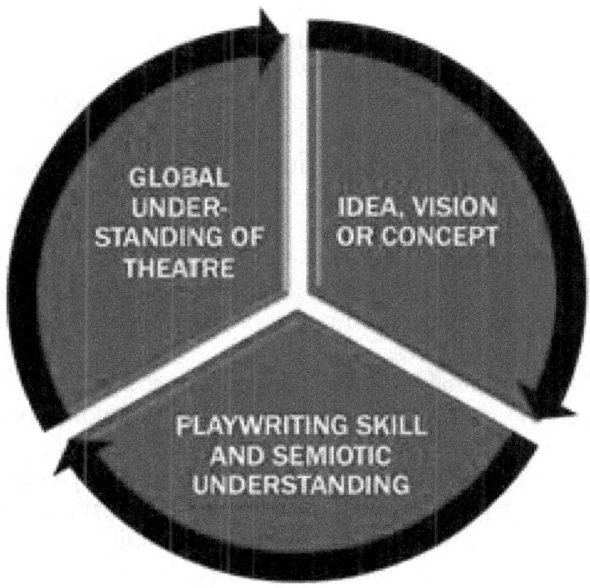

Figure 6.4 Components of a playwriting student

watching theatre being performed. A number of teachers mentioned the students' exposure to theatre as key to their understanding of how to write a play (Mr P from St Anne's and Ms S from GLC). In terms of the student participants in my research, on the whole the students had quite well-developed appreciating skills. Most were able to discuss the plays they had seen or read with, at times, sophisticated theatre literacy and insight.

The next two components are closely interlinked and it is here that opportunities for skill and knowledge development are yet to be fully realised. The second aspect I have termed their 'creativity', that is the idea or concept put forth. Developing the vision of the play, the ideas to be explored, the world the students want to create and the impetus for writing is a process, and one that can be actively taught. The third aspect is their playwriting skills or understanding of the language of plays or theatre semiotics. The ability to think metaphorically, and to develop an idea and transform it into motifs or symbols, is a skill that enables the students to turn their idea or vision from a concept to a performable text. It involves the students knowing how to control the elements of drama in the temporal reality of the stage: dialogue, setting, suspense, subtext, conflict, complications, relationships.

An understanding of the relationship between these three components is important in recognising the teachers' role in the creative process. Amabile (1996) describes three necessary aspects for circumstances to be conducive to creativity – task motivation, the domain of relevant skills and creativity-relevant processes. The focus now turns to what strategies teachers can use to improve both domain of specific skills and creativity processes.

As Csikszentmihalyi (2008) suggests, it is the students' increasing skill that will allow them to attain flow, achieve autotelic motivation, and enable them to meet the challenge of the task. In this section I argue that a student's playwriting skill can be explicitly taught and developed through understanding of the semiotics of the stage. In turn, there is evidence to suggest that this increased skill will also feed their creativity and open them to new forms of expression.

Semiotics and creativity

As the dramatic text makes use of 'verbal . . . visual and acoustic codes' (Pfister, 1988) a strong 'dramatic literacy' or ability to 'speak' the language of the stage is necessary to equip the students with the skills to write. This literacy, like language, is more than appreciating theatre – the realm of the global understanding – but involves being able to 'code' their own ideas to be read and understood by others. Learning to understand and manipulate 'imaginative shorthand' (Smiley 2005, 160), the signs and symbols that constitute stage language, will give the students a greater vocabulary and aesthetic control. To achieve this, teachers may need to extend their teaching and learning activities in their playwriting classroom to more closely resemble their normal drama classroom. They need to go beyond suggestions of plays to read, to the explicit deconstruction of plays and genres – to see 'how' meaning is made in a variety of contexts and world views, and explore experimentation with these forms before a student emotionally commits to an idea. While this is a slight change in focus it could result in significant improvements in the students' independence in the process. To provide the students with tools for theatrical thinking and expressing, the playwriting teacher will need to teach the meanings of these codes, signs, and symbols as part of, not after, the idea-generation phase.

I am arguing that there is evidence to suggest that knowledge improves creativity in much the same way as vocabulary increases thought. In language, the greater number of words you have in your bank, the more diverse and sophisticated your thinking can be, to quote Wittgenstein, 'the limits of my language means the limits of my world' (Wittgenstein 1922). As Nicholson (1998) argues, greater knowledge of the theatrical codes will give the students an 'expanded cultural field' and thus opportunity for thought previously 'inconceivable'. As students gain new modes of expression, Nicholson argues, 'this will not only extend their creativity, it will enhance their conceptual development' (1998, 79). Rather than corrupting the students' voice, as the noble savage concept supposes, knowledge of a wide variety of styles, techniques and conventions (as tools to be employed, not rules to be obeyed) should be enabling.

A writer needs to understand the 'old' to reinterpret it to make something new. As Gombrich (1966) argues, each 'work is related by imitation or contradiction to what has come before' (3). Kushner concurs: 'by all means ... invent something new, but know where you are coming from, who built the stage you walk out onto' (Herrington & Brian 2006, 146). As does Waters: 'No one since Aeschylus wrote a play without seeing or reading another one' (2012, 5). This emphasis on continuity reinforces our need to reject the belief in the mystical Muse and recognise that creativity requires structure and methodology; that 'the intangible creative state requires order so that the artist may then put form to his vision' (Hardy 1993, 67).

Role of the teacher

How then should a teacher approach this refocusing of the teacher–student dynamic? To enable the 'refocus' the teacher may need to rethink their role. The majority of the teaching input in the classrooms I studied took the form of 'negative instruction' (Selden 1946) where the students submit drafts and the teacher critiques their work 'finding faults to be rectified'. This problematisation approach, while necessary at times, must be handled skilfully, as it has the potential to create an unproductive dynamic. Starko (2005) describes two types of feedback: controlling, which positions the teacher as arbiter of good and bad, and informational, which encourages autonomy, gives information on what is successful and provides gauges for self-assessment. Problematisation is therefore most effective in the context of greater input – which challenges the noble savage approach to pedagogy. If the student perceives the teacher as the 'critic', the students then see the teacher as the one who can tell them what is wrong with their play and how to fix it. Furthermore, if the majority of feedback takes the form of annotated drafts, rather than discussion after workshop performances, then the primacy of the teacher is reinforced. My suggestion is that we need to rethink the relationship, and rather see our role as a dramaturg, one who can build the potential, identify possibilities, and not merely one that highlights flaws. The play should then not be problematised but analysed. As Smiley (2005) elaborates, analysis means separating the whole into parts and studying those parts and their relationships, whereas criticism frequently amounts to adverse commentary regarding faults and shortcomings.

The practice of playwriting instruction would be improved if problems and strengths were identified in a moved reading so the student had an opportunity to see what was and wasn't working, and can receive feedback from the audience and the teacher. This situation allows the teacher to be an expert advisor, but not the sole arbiter of the play's success or failure. The distinction here is an important one and is explained best by thinking about where the teacher is positioned. Where does the teacher 'sit' in the theatre when they engage with the play, in the audience as a critic or backstage with the writer?

In terms of flow, identifying problems within the text without providing the input that would allow students to solve these problems, does not provide the students with the opportunity to develop the skills needed to meet the increasingly complex challenge of playwriting. 'Problematisation' then works to focus students on what they can't do or haven't done. In my research, a number of students 'flew out' of the flow channel as the challenge outstripped their skill, and thus disengaged from ownership of the task. As the deadline approached, the students began to rely more heavily on teacher input implicitly and explicitly requesting specific suggestions for improvment. Given the problematisation dynamic that had been established, many of the teachers found themselves having to be more direct in the offering of solutions to the problems they had themselves identified (Ms S, Mr P and Ms J). This situation is not satisfying for the teacher or the student, and may go some way to explaining the trepidation felt by teachers.

While some problematisation is often unavoidable, an approach which in more time is spent working with the student to develop a theatrical idea before the first draft and to equip them with the semiotic language of the stage as they develop their vision, could minimise the paralysis and provide the student with the skills to experiment with form and the theatrical devices to improve their piece. A response to these issues is one of refocusing. The role of the teacher could be more effective with a focus on dramaturgy not criticism, and on teaching students the craft of playwriting through semiotics and genre study. Subsequently, we need to rethink the wisdom of the noble savage model of creative mentoring, as this idea paradoxically limits the student's ability to reach their potential.

Implications for policy and further research

The benefits of playwriting go beyond the confines of the drama classroom. There is emerging evidence that playwriting programs are uniquely placed to provide authentic and engaging opportunities for the development of literacy skills (Chizhik 2009; Gardiner & Anderson 2012) and that students, particularly marginalised students, experience increased feelings of efficacy (Feffer 2009) and inclusion (Fisher 2008). However, as the evidence emerges of the need to embrace the art form and capitalise on the pastoral and theatrical benefits it promotes, it is clear that many drama teachers are avoiding teaching the craft because of its perceived difficulty.

This chapter has provided evidence that a renewed focus on teaching and learning, and a new concept of creativity, could address the factors that have contributed to disengagement in students and feelings of inadequacy in teachers. This approach, which goes beyond the noble savage paradigm, could lead to a more enjoyable and rewarding experience for both, where teacher and student achieve greater proficiency. This also draws attention to the need for more professional learning in playwriting teaching, for both pre-service and experienced teachers. It is vital to ensure a sustained culture of performance writing in schools, and for the future of Australian performance writing. But it is more important to provide an engaging and realistic writing experience for students to have their voices heard, and to encourage diversity and democracy of these voices, both in content and form. While more research is needed, the emerging findings from my study suggest that playwriting is uniquely placed to provide that avenue. However, as the original provocation of this chapter suggested, more research is needed to determine the best playwriting approach for each stage of learning – from preschool to pre-service teachers.

Conclusion

As we are simultaneously teaching the rules and encouraging innovation, drama teachers need to adopt a pedagogical approach that takes account of the spectrum of theoretical approaches for two main reasons. Firstly, it will extend the students' understanding of what a play can be and broaden their semiotic vocabulary, which has the potential to encourage creativity and innovation in their writing. Secondly, it will broaden the teachers' view of what a play is, and should equip teachers with the skills to identify innovation and encourage individual voice, rather than restrict the student's voice by applying generic categories.

Developments in playwriting and creativity theory suggest that the imagination needs structure (Hardy 1993), and that the more students know about the semiotics of playwriting the more creative they will be (Nicholson 1998). The current approach, that minimises teaching activities and focuses on problematisation, has the potential to stifle rather than unleash the unique voice of the student playwright. It is also clear that playwriting pedagogy has much to learn from creativity theory, especially the flow experience, which could have a significant positive impact on the way we teach playwriting in the classroom. The refocusing of the student–teacher dynamic, from critic to dramaturg, could see a much more rewarding experience for both teacher and student, resulting in more autonomy in the student and a more satisfying teaching experience for the teacher.

Acknowledgments

I would like to acknowledge and thank Michael Anderson and Kelly Freebody, my doctoral supervisors, for their guidance and assistance in the preparation of this chapter.

Works cited

Amabile TM (1996). *Creativity in context*. Boulder, CO: Westview Press.
Anderson M (2012). *Masterclass in drama education: transforming teaching and learning*. London: Continuum.
Aristotle (1996). *Poetics*. M Heath, Trans. London: Penguin Classics.
Castagno P (1993). Informing the new dramaturgy: critical theory to creative process. *Theatre Topics*, 3(1): pp29–42.
Castagno P (2001). *New playwriting strategies: a language based approach to playwriting*. New York: Routledge.
Catron LE (2002). *The elements of playwriting*. Long Grove, IL: Waveland Press, Inc.
Chizhik A W (2009). Literacy for playwriting or playwriting for literacy. *Education and Urban Society*, 41(3): pp387–409
Csikszentmihalyi M (1993). Activity and happiness: toward a science of occupation. *Occupational Science: Australia*, 1(1): pp38–42.
Csikszentmihalyi M (2008). *Flow: the psychology of optimal experience*. New York: Harper Perennial Modern Classics.
Csikszentmihalyi M, Rathunde K & Whalen S (1993). *Talented teenagers: the roots of success and failure*. New York: Cambridge University Press.
Edgar D (2009). *How plays work*. London: Nick Hearn Books.
Egri L (1960). *The art of dramatic writing*. New York: Simon and Schuster.
Ellingson T (2001). *The myth of the noble savage*. Berkley: University of California Press.
Esslin M (1965). Introduction. In M Esslin *Absurd drama* (pp7–23). London: Penguin Books.
Feffer LB (2009). Devising ensemble plays: at risk students becoming living, performing authors. *English Journal*, 98(3): pp46–52.
Fisher MT (2008). Catching butterflies. *English Education*, 40(2): pp94–100

Freytag G (1900). *Technique of the drama: an exposition of dramatic composition and art.* EJ MacEwan, Trans. Chicago: Scott, Foresman and Company.

Gardiner P & Anderson M (2012). Can you read that again? Playwriting, literacy and reading the spoken word. *English in Australia,* 47(2): pp80–89.

Gombrich EH (1966). *The story of art.* London: Phaidon.

Greer S (1993). The noble savage. *Winds of Change,* 8(2): pp89–92.

Hardy J (1993). *Development of playwriting theory: demonstrated in two original scripts.* Lubbock, Texas: Texas Tech University.

Herrington J & Brian C (Eds) (2006). *Playwrights teach playwriting: revealing essays by contemporary playwrights.* Hanover, NH: Smith and Kraus.

Jackson M (2001). Ter Ellingson. The myth of the noble savage. *Utopian Studies,* 12(2): pp292

Jensen J (1997). Playwriting quick and dirty. *The Writer,* 110(9): pp10–13.

McIntyre P (2012). *Creativity and cultural production.* New York: Palgrave Macmillan.

McKean B (2007). Composition in theatre: writing and devising performance. In L Bresler (Ed.) *International handbook of research in arts education.* Dordrecht: Springer: pp503–15

Nicholson H (1998). Writing plays: taking note of genre. In D Hornbrook (Ed.), *On the subject of drama.* New York: Routledge: pp73–91

Norden B (2007). How to write a play: or, can creative writing be taught? *Third Text,* 21(5): 643–48.

Pfister,M (1988). *The theory and analysis of drama.* Cambridge: Cambridge University Press.

Selden S (1946). *An introduction to playwriting.* New York: F S Crofts and Co., Inc.

Smiley S (2005). *Playwriting: the structure of action.* New Haven and London: Yale University Press.

Starko AJ (2005). *Creativity in the classroom: schools of curious delight.* 3rd edn. Mahwah, NY; London: Lawrence Erlbaum Associates.

Stephenson H & Langridge N (Eds) (1997). *Rage and reason: women playwrights on playwriting.* London: Methuen Drama.

Waters S (2012). *The secret life of plays.* London: Nick Hern Books.

Waxberg CS (1998). *The actor's script: script analysis for performers.* Portsmouth, NH: Heinemann.

Wittgenstein L (1922). *Tractatus logico-philosophicus.* London: Kegan Paul, Trench, Trubner & Co.

7
The drama of co-intentional dialogue: reflections on the confluent praxis of Dorothy Heathcote and Paulo Freire

Gerard Boland

Dorothy Heathcote (1926–2011) and Paulo Freire (1921–1997) were generational contemporaries. The learning and teaching propositions that they developed and championed were truly revolutionary, for both called into question the efficacy of transmission pedagogy as the prevailing orthodox for teaching practice. Even when inquiry methods began to gain favour in Australian tertiary faculties of education during the 1970s, the epistemological propositions put forward by Dorothy Heathcote and Paulo Freire retained their unique resonances as counterpoint perspectives which resolutely placed the student's 'thought-language-context' (Freire 1998a, 141) at the centre of every educational project. In taking this approach both emphasised very concrete, practical means by which teachers could – and should – reframe the learning encounter in order to privilege democratic values and directly share the 'power to tell' (Heathcote 1984f, 164) with the learner-participants by actively working to resolve what Paulo Freire called the 'teacher-student contradiction' (1994b, 53–56).

In making their pioneering innovations during the 1950s and 1960s both Heathcote and Freire used their academic appointments

---

Boland G (2015). The drama of co-intentional dialogue: reflections on the confluent praxis of Dorothy Heathcote and Paulo Freire. In M Anderson & C Roche (Eds). *The state of the art: teaching drama in the 21st century*, (129–148). Sydney: Sydney University Press.

within universities and other institutions as a base from which to test their ideas and share their insights with local educators. Their approaches represented serious challenges to the comfortable assumptions of transmission pedagogy, and gained national, and then international attention as each conducted workshops and seminars, and began to publish papers that put forth compelling propositions for problem-based approaches to learning and teaching. These efforts had a snowball effect that eventually brought their ideas to a vast international audience. Both Freire and Heathcote made their first visits to Australia during the mid-1970s. Their international audience of educators grew to include professionals drawn from many other disciplines, and in time, the growing appreciation of the potency and originality of their epistemological propositions began to attract commentary that sought to explain why, and explore how, these propositions represented such a radical departure from not only transmission pedagogy, but inquiry methods as well. The discussion offered here reflects upon the state of our art by presenting aspects of that debate to a new generation of Australian educators who did not have direct access – as students – to either of these individuals, but who nevertheless have an to opportunity to encounter them in a direct way through their video recordings and written texts, as well as through the testimony of those who seized the opportunity to undertake a period of study with them.

Assessing the current state of any social movement offers a Janus-like moment in which we can pause to look both backward and forward in time. In doing so it becomes possible to notice that different generations undertake different types of tasks. Often these are most clearly perceived in the rear vision mirror of history, but sometimes these tasks are well understood by those who collaborate to accomplish group-defined goals. The generational task of those Australian drama educators who have recently retired or are now moving toward the conclusion of their working lives was to create the different state-based drama curricula and establish state and national organisations to serve as vehicles for political advocacy and as a means for enhancing communication amongst and between Australian teachers and like-minded colleagues overseas.

Yet further tasks remain. One of these is to develop a more comprehensive account of the epistemological schemes that animated the desire to engage in this particular form of 'cultural action' (Freire 1972a,

7 The drama of co-intentional dialogue

76–77) by identifying and reassessing the philosophical influences that informed and motivated the development of the drama in education movement in Australia. This is a task for contemporary theorist/practitioners. How did influences drawn from educational philosophy and educational psychology resonate with a growing awareness of the works of Peter Slade, Brian Way, Richard Courtney, Gavin Bolton or Dorothy Heathcote? The analysis offered here explores how Dorothy Heathcote's approach to drama in education parallels and exemplifies the central epistemological ideas articulated by Paulo Freire. Drawing attention to their syncretic propositions is intended to initiate discussion about the relation between larger international discourses and the works of drama in education practitioners, whose insights influenced the development of drama curricula and theatre in education practice in Australia.

Much has been written about how drama-based learning and teaching might be transacted. Likewise, much has been published concerning what should be taught in terms of syllabus selection. Finding satisfactory answers to these questions were – and are – essential to establishing and sustaining the vigour of well-designed drama curricula and progressing the ongoing debate about curriculum development among the membership of our state and national organisations.

A consideration of why the dimension of the issue has produced landmark studies (Little 1983; Schaffner 1986; Carroll 1980, 1986b, 1988) that offered quantifiable research conclusions, that demonstrated that language use within the 'drama framework' (Carroll 1980, 20; Heathcote 1984f, 168) produces new types of learning when compared to more traditional classroom interactions. Here neither the teachers nor the students alter their normative social roles in order to reflect upon learning content by thinking and speaking from the worldview of assumed fictional roles. The focus of this inquiry lies in drawing attention to the ways in which Dorothy Heathcote's process-driven approach to learning and teaching – through the use of 'teacher in role' and 'mantle of the expert' drama – exemplifies Paulo Freire's conceptualisation of the conscientisation process (*conscientização*).

The state of the art

An epistemological proposition

We are really asking an epistemological question when we inquire into the ways in which conventional approaches to teacher–student communication are altered when in-role communication is used to contemplate, examine, and decode dramatic 'role conventions' (Heathcote 1984f, 166–67). The use of full role, attitudinal role and secondary role conventions calls upon students to interrogate different types of information about learning content from a point of view that is quite different from those which they typically experience in either transmission-oriented or inquiry-based classrooms. That is, we are asking, what is 'the nature of the relationship between the knower (the inquirer) and the known (or knowable)'? (Guba 1990, 18). The Greek linguistic roots for 'epistemology' reveal nuanced shades of meaning that remain embedded within the modern word, and these are worth (re)considering:

> episteme knowledge, understanding, from epistanai, to stand upon, understand: epi– upon + histanai, to stand, place. (Morris 1970, 441)

It is in this foundation-like place to stand upon – in order to gain understanding – that we should consider the epistemological assumptions which guide a dialogical, problem-based approach to nurturing educational environments, in which the growth of a 'critical being' (Barnett 1997, 103) becomes possible as we labour to design sturdy yet responsive structures for learning through the use of in-role communication with our students.

These possibilities are succinctly presented in John Carroll's important illustration (Figure 7.1), which depicts how different role positions work to establish varied points of view, providing both 'distance' and 'protection' in relation to how a dramatically framed event can focus the attention of the learner-participants upon new types of inductive learning.

This orientation around inductive learning arises precisely because 'role-shifted discourse' enables the participants 'to take control of the [drama-based] interaction through their language initiatives' (Carroll 1988, 20). It is in this sense that 'role-shifted discourse' presents new epistemic opportunities and questions about the relationship between 'the knower' and 'the known', which can be 'framed' and 'reframed'

7 The drama of co-intentional dialogue

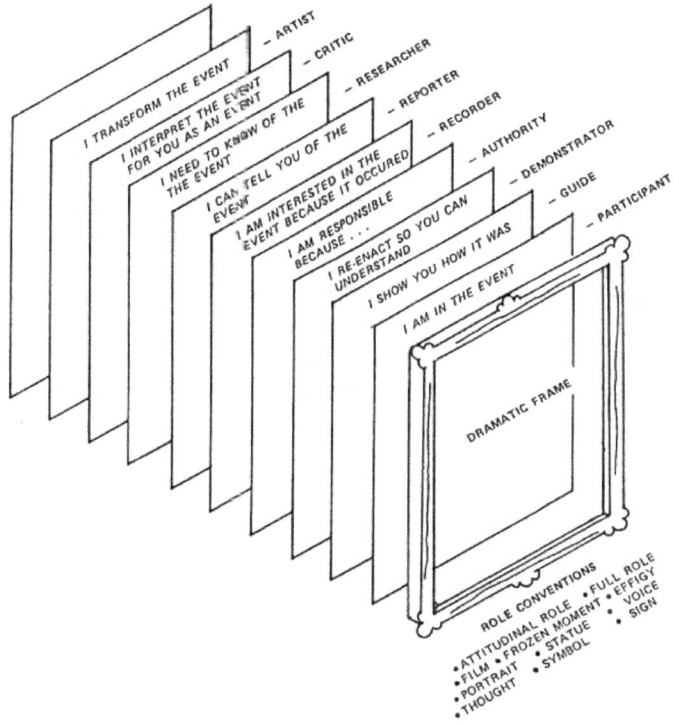

Figure 7.1 Role distance (Carroll 1986a, 6; 1986b, 125)

(Goffman 1974; Heathcote 1984f) according to the choices negotiated and adopted by the teacher in dialogue with the learner-participants.

Our place to stand – our vantage point from which to work with students so they might gain an understanding of using performative, role-based communication, for engaging with any curricular content – cannot be located solely within the normative processual practices of either transmission or inquiry-based pedagogies. For both transmission and inquiry orientations tend to place the control of the pace of the learning, and especially the motivating locus of authority, with the teacher.

Drama teachers know that working in-role from within the 'drama framework' specifically empowers them to temporarily set aside the normative expectations that students project upon them concerning the notion that they – as teachers – would (naturally) know the answers to the questions that the students might put to them, or that they would (naturally) know the answers to all the questions which they might put to the students (see Heathcote 1984b, 85–87). Interacting with students from within the 'drama framework' enables teachers to select roles that position themselves with a low status and limited authority, or roles that might plausibly exhibit a distinct lack of information or knowledge concerning the questions which confront the students as they attempt to solve those issues from the point of view of their assumed roles.

The act of assuming a fictional role re-frames the participants' normative expectations concerning their relationship with the subject content under investigation, as well as with one another and their teacher within the learning and teaching encounter. The 'drama framework' re-orders the status and authority of their actual social roles as teachers and students (Heathcote 1984f, 161–65) by requiring the learner-participants to solve the problems and questions which attend those issues in ways that are consistent with, and relevant to, the 'dramatic pretext' (O'Neill 1995, 20) of their in-role interactions with one another. For these fictional challenges exist to authenticate a situated, depictive context that can enable the learner-participants to generate – and test – the new knowledge that they are called upon to inductively reason in consequence of the ways in which 'mantle of the expert' drama (Heathcote 1984a, 205–7) supports and facilitates their use of both in-role and out-of-role dialogue to resolve the 'dramatic tension' (Heathcote 1984e, 130–31) and dilemmas that have been introduced and developed by their interactions with one another. And, significantly, their 'role-shifted discourse' concretely demonstrates that the 'drama framework' can be a very effective means of resolving many of the negative effects that accrue from what Paulo Freire characterises as the 'teacher–student contradiction' (1994b, 53–56).

Drama practitioners – as teachers who use different types of dramatic activity such as exercise, dramatic playing and theatre (Bolton 1979, 2), as well as different styles of process drama (O'Neill & Lambert 1982; O'Neill 1995; Bolton & Heathcote 1999; Neelands & Goode 2000)

7 The drama of co-intentional dialogue

to teach any curriculum content – will recognise and understand why Paulo Freire avers that:

> Reading the world always precedes reading the word, and reading the word implies continually reading the world ... this movement from the word to the world is always present; even the spoken word flows from our reading of the world. In a way, however, we can go further and say that reading the word is not preceded merely by reading the world, but by a certain form of writing it or rewriting it, that is, of transforming it by means of conscious, practical work. For me, this dynamic movement is central to the literacy process ... Words should be laden with the meaning of the people's existential experience, and not of the teacher's experience ... (Freire & Macedo 1987, 35)

My proposition is that Freire's perspectives concerning the ways in which cultural literacies are developed by 'reading the world' and 'naming the world' (Freire 1994b, 69) are highly relevant to the ways in which drama teachers can reflect upon their lesson planning. This is never more apparent than when we choose to employ Heathcote's 'role conventions' (1984f, 166–67) as embodied forms of selective 'signing' to reframe the social context for learning and teaching as an 'intersubjective' (Freire 1998a, 136) opportunity for 'role-shifted discourse' within our classrooms.

We would do well to recognise that the 'role conventions' that Dorothy Heathcote enumerated in *Signs and portents* (1984f, 160–69) represent what Paulo Freire's called 'compound codifications' (1994b, 104; 1972a, 32). His advice is to employ 'compound codifications' that will function as the central value/means for guiding and sustaining a deepening the dialogue on the part of learner-participants in wanting to solve realistic problems that enable them to use their knowledge for those situated purposes. As Freire observed, 'it is to the reality which mediates men, and to the perception of that reality held by educators and people, that we must go to find the program content of education' (1994b, 77). So let us now dig a little deeper into Paulo Freire's thinking about the nature of what a 'conscientising praxis' means within the context of the learning encounter. In particular, by examining how the characteristics that define the phases of his *conscientização* process are present within Dorothy Heathcote's approach to drama in education, and how both offer guidance for drama teachers who wish to utilise 'problem-posing' questions (Freire 1994b, 60–64) as the principal value/means for facilitating dialogue with students in order to critically interrogate curriculum content while developing their individual analytical and improvisational skills, and their group work skills.

Agents of their own learning

'The starting point for organising the program content of education' says Paulo Freire, 'must be the present, existential, concrete situation, reflecting the aspirations of the people'; and one which uses 'the thought-language with which men and women refer to reality, the levels at which they perceive that reality, and their view of the world, in which their generative themes are found' (1994b, 77–8). His comments about 'the starting point' for learning and teaching emphasise his uncompromising adherence to the epistemological value(s) of student-centred education, for his 'problem-posing' approach to dialogue empowers the participants to engage a group-defined 'educational project' (1994b, 36) that takes their 'thought-language' about their 'situationality' as the starting point. 'Reflection upon situationality' he says, 'is reflection about the very condition of existence: critical thinking by means of which people discover each other to be "in a situation" ' (1994b, 90).

The key to understanding the conceptual links between Paulo Freire's *conscientização* process (1973b, 23; 1998a, 49–52; 1996, 127–34) and Dorothy Heathcote's approach to drama in education lies in their procedural orientation toward privileging 'co-intentional' 'problem-posing' dialogue within the classroom (Freire 1994b, 51, 53). Both emphasise the need to investigate the 'thought-language-context' (Freire 1998a, 141) of the learner-participants and then honour their input by 'putting the students' point of view to work' (Heathcote 1984d, 44). Both Heathcote and Freire insisted, and consistently demonstrated, how the learning encounter needs to be constructed around the 'thematic universe' (Freire 1994b, 90) of the learners who simultaneously engage with the teacher to enlarge and transform their understanding of the drama-based project of the moment, or the socio-historic dimension of the curriculum content under consideration.

7 The drama of co-intentional dialogue

Freire's epistemological proposition relates to what he called the 'gnosiological cycle' of learning, meaning for him 'the cycle of the act of knowing, the relation between knowing existing knowledge and producing new knowledge' (Paulo Freire in Shor & Freire 1987, 151). Returning to this topic in his posthumously published book, *Pedagogy of freedom: ethics, democracy, and civic courage* (1998b), he reminded his readers once again that 'co-intentional' education:

> requires the existence of 'subjects,' who while teaching, learn. And who in learning also teach. The reciprocal learning between teachers and students is what gives educational practice its gnostic character. (Freire 1998b, 67)

The connection between these Freirean epistemic propositions and Dorothy Heathcote's approach to drama in education – in terms of the ways in which she proposes the use of 'teacher in role' and 'mantle of the expert' – is that both represent a 'permanent movement of searching [that] creates a capacity for learning not only in order to adapt to the world but especially to intervene, to re-create, and to transform it' (Freire 1998b, 66). Considered from this point of view the primary role of teachers revolves around our adroit employment of 'problem-posing' dialogue to enlarge the students' collective capacity to inductively generate new knowledge – irrespective of whether or not that new knowledge represents either discrete or blended expressions of affective, psychomotor or cognitive reasoning (Bloom 1956–64; Anderson & Sosniak 1994).

I turn now to a discussion of the *conscientização* process in which Paulo Freire's own voice is foregrounded in order to give a more direct appreciation of how he explained his approach to learning and teaching, and to enable readers to more clearly perceive the theoretical/conceptual connections of the conscientisation process with Dorothy Heathcote's approach to drama in education.

The conscientisation process (*conscientização*)

The *conscientização* process is founded in 'educational projects' (Freire 1994b, 36) that begin with an investigation of the themes that shape people's perceptions about the 'thought-language-context' of their own life situation (Freire 1998a, 141). The purpose of the *conscientização* process is to reveal the presence of 'knowing Subject[s]' (Freire 1973b, 24) to one another in ways that enable them to perceive their relationships with one another in new, more critical ways, so that – within the drama frame at least – they can act to transform limiting aspects of the situated social context that their assumed roles inhabit (1994b, 80). This requires communication that is formed around modalities of 'intersubjective dialogue' (1994b, 116–17; 1998a, 136) that are all too frequently absent from communication between teachers and students in transmission-based classrooms with its emphasis upon procedural information and discussion of objective facts relating to the material world (Carroll 1986b, 206; 1988, 16, 20).

'It is not our role' as educators, Freire says:

> to speak to the people about our own view of the world nor attempt to impose that view on them, but rather to dialogue with the people about their view and ours. We must realise that their view of the world, manifested variously in their action, reflects their situation in the world. (1994b, 77)

The role of the dialogical educator is, therefore, to investigate the 'thematic universe' of the students and then to 're-present it not as a lecture, but as a problem' (1994b, 90). 'The program content of the problem-posing method' he says:

> is constituted and organised by the students' view of the world, where their own generative themes are found. The content thus constantly expands and renews itself. (Freire, 1994b, 9)

Or, as Heathcote consistently emphasised over many years, '[p]eople have to employ what they already know, about the [fictional] life they are trying to live ... drama puts life experience to use' (1984a, 204). Within the 'drama framework' people are encouraged and empowered to externalise their own reflections by assuming fictional roles that use symbolic languages to construct embodied codifications which depict their 'reading [of] the world'. These readings emerge through shared 'intersubjective' dialogues that enable the learner-participants within

7 The drama of co-intentional dialogue

the drama to define and construct 'compound codifications' that put their own 'life experiences to use' through their depictive actions within the context of a drama (as an enacted episode or exercise-based improvisation). Assisting students to codify the 'thought-language-context' of their reflections upon the social reality of their assumed roles enables the learner-participants to reflexively consider their role-based experiences as 'an object to be thought about' (Shor & Freire 1987, 40). This activity provides the safety of 'a no penalty area, using people in groups, in immediate contextual time' (Heathcote 1984e, 130) in order to consider diverse issues and ethical problems in terms of the viewpoint of the student's assumed role:

> If it is in speaking their word that people, by naming the world, transform it, [then] dialogue imposes itself as the way by which they achieve significance as human beings. Dialogue is thus an existential necessity. And since dialogue is the encounter in which the united reflection and action of the dialoguers are addressed to the world which is to be transformed and humanised, this dialogue cannot be reduced to the act of one person's 'depositing' ideas in another, nor can it become a simple exchange of ideas to be 'consumed' by the discussants. (Freire 1994b, 59–70)

This is an important concept in terms of Freire's epistemological propositions concerning the *conscientização* process. We teachers work to enhance the learner-participants' claim on critical and creative agency to define the expressive character of their engagement of drama processes through the different types of 'co-intentional' actions/interactions we utilise in order to assist them to identify the 'significant themes on the basis of which the program content of [their] education can be built' (Freire 1994b, 74–74). Both Heathcote and Freire emphasise the necessity of investigating the 'thought-language' that students use to describe their perceptions of the world because through their very activity in this naming, we begin to humanise the world, so that the collaborative, dialogical activity in the work of this 'naming' transforms our perception in favour of seeing ourselves as the subject of the learning and not merely the object of some type of externally defined curriculum outcome. We must not, says Freire, surrender to others the right to name our 'significant themes' nor should we cede all decision-making agency by permitting others to define the entirety of the program content of our learning for us.

> Critics of such an approach might begin to worry about the program ... I say to them that I am not against a curriculum or a program, but only against the authoritarian and elitist ways of organising the studies. I am defending the critical participation of the students in their education. (Shor & Freire 1987, 107)

For Paulo Freire, men and women are 'beings of praxis' who reveal different modalities of consciousness in their relationship with the social and natural world (1994b, 106; 1998a, 111). 'Knowing' he says, 'is the task of Subjects, not of objects. It is as a Subject, and only as such, that a man or woman can really know' (1998a, 101). Educators who embrace these epistemological perspectives and ontological values must determine to resolve the 'teacher–student contradiction' as a necessary first step in order to alter the power dynamics within the social encounters that occur between themselves and the participants within any learning and teaching interaction that is conducted as an improvisation activity, an episode of process drama, or as a theatre-making enterprise. A 'problem-posing' approach to dialogical learning and teaching can be carried out in any educational context, and critical thinking, when expressed as 'intersubjective dialogue', will tend to be multidisciplinary.

Dialogue that is conducted with the aim of enabling people to 'name the world' (Freire 1994b, 69, 83) works to affirm our shared historical and 'ontological vocation' to 'become more fully human' (1994b, 26, 55). Freire emphasised this point again and again throughout his life:

> When I insist on dialogical education starting from the students' comprehension of their daily life experiences, no matter if they are students of the university or kids in primary school or workers in a neighbourhood or peasants in the countryside, my insistence on starting from their description of their daily life experiences is based in the possibility of starting from concreteness, from common sense, to reach a rigorous understanding of reality. (Shor & Freire 1987, 106)

7 The drama of co-intentional dialogue

Freire and his confederates experimented with an educational innovation 'which would be the instrument of the learner as well as of the educator'; one which 'would identify learning content with the learning process' (1998a, 48–49). The literacy program that Freire describes in the chapter entitled 'Education as the practice of freedom' in *Education for critical consciousness* (1998a), and in chapter three of *Pedagogy of the oppressed* (1994b), concerns the activity of teams of educators who enter local communities in order to discover the thematic concerns of the adult students who will participate in the literacy program. In doing so these educators begin to understand the ways in which these themes and issues are manifested in the 'thought-language' (1994b, 77–78) of people's daily lives.

The theoretical/conceptual categories for describing the *conscientização* process are embedded within Freire's discussion of the phases of *conscientização* process throughout several of his early books; in particular, *Cultural action for freedom* (1972a), *Pedagogy of the oppressed* (1972c), and *Education for critical consciousness* (1974). Table 7.1 was constructed using insights drawn from an explanatory analysis developed by Denis Collins (1977, 83) and uses Freire's own writing to clarify and amplify my discussion of conscientisation as a process of investigation, thematisation, problematisation and cultural intervention. It constructs a portrait of what I call the action-progressions of the *conscientização* process in a way that illuminates Freire's emphasis on the 'problem-posing' dimension of dialogical education in terms that are integral to both his own adult literacy projects and the conduct of 'educational projects' which reflect the process-based insights offered by Dorothy Heathcote's approach to utilising 'teacher in role' and/or 'mantle of the expert' drama for learning and teaching.

The principle contribution that Table 7.1 makes to the work of illuminating Freirean epistemology lies in the way in which his concepts concerning the *conscientização* process are presented in a synoptic fashion that is both simple and direct in its expression. Rendered in this way it becomes possible to hold these guiding principles in mind while collaborating with others to co-intentionally construct new meanings, and define new drama-based applications from the conceptual expressions that Freire used to describe the learning and teaching dimensions of his approach to conscientisation.

Table 7.1 Education for critical literacy: Paulo Freire's *conscientização* process and in-role communication within Dorothy Heathcote's conceptualisation of the drama frame

Investigation	Dialogue to discover the words that describe the 'thought-language-context' (Freire 1998a, 141) of the learner-participants' existing knowledge and skills concerning the social, technical and environmental context of the drama; the discovery of their 'generative words' (1998a, 50–55) enables participants to use the drama frame to reflexively interrogate their perceptions as a 'living code to be deciphered' (1994b, 92).
Thematisation	Identification of the 'generative themes' (1994b, 77–78, 84–85, 90) of the drama participants is achieved through dialogue aimed at the 'reduction/coding/decoding' (1998a, 51; 1994b, 96, 98–100, 102) of their 'meaningful thematics' (1994b, 93). Generative themes 'are set into codifications' (1998a, 51) through embodied and depictive conventions of role and role distance, variously framed as full role, attitudinal role, and/or diverse conventions of secondary role (Heathcote 1984f, 166–67). Issues emerge as a 'thematic fan' (1994b, 96) which reveal a 'complex of interacting themes' (1994b, 83) which the learner-participants engage through diverse modalities of in-role and out-of-role dialogue.
Problematisation	Identification of 'limit situations' and 'limit acts' (1994b, 80, 83, 94) as 'coded situation-problems' (1998a, 51) that contain myths (1972a, 30; 1973a, 25; 1994b, 120–21) and contradiction (1994b, 93–94) relating to the unique living code of the life of the area (1994b, 92) in which the participants of the drama interact. 'Dialogical intersubjectivity' (1998a, 136) amongst 'thematic investigation circles' (1994b, 98) of learner-participants who are endowed with adult expertise, facilitates their identification of 'hinged themes' (1994b, 101); naïve perceptions become critical 'as potential consciousness supersedes real consciousness' and the learner-participants begin to appreciate changes in their understanding as a critical 'perception of their previous perception' (1994b, 96) that allows them to articulate new agendas for problematising the themes and tasks that inhere to the satisfactory working out of their drama.
Cultural intervention	'These contradictions [concerning the 'coded situation-problem'] constitute limit-situations, involve themes, and indicate tasks' (1994b, 94). These tasks involve 'intervention in the

7 The drama of co-intentional dialogue

> world as transformers of that world' (1994b, 54) and are based upon 'an attitude of creation and re-creation, of self-transformation producing a stance of intervention in one's context' (1998a, 48) through the application of 'dialogical action' that is realised through cooperation (1994b, 148–53), 'unity for liberation' (1994b, 153–56), organisation (1994b, 156–60), and 'cultural synthesis' (1994b, 160–64) as both out-of-role classroom participants and as in-role collaborators who interact within the fictional drama frame.

Table 7.1 contributes to international discourses concerning Freire and his conceptualisation of the *conscientização* process because it provides a précis of his learning and teaching process, and underscores the ontological values upon which his central epistemological insights are constructed. Remarkably, this is somewhat unusual in the context of the literature devoted to analysing Paulo Freire's educational insights, for instead of offering an interpretive commentary on what I believe Freire means, what is offered here is a succinct, closely cross-referenced profile of the language that Freire himself used to explain and define the phases of the *conscientização* process in terms of the way that it illuminates the role-based innovations in learning and teaching that Dorothy Heathcote pioneered.

What Heathcote understood is that the act of inhabiting a role – as a persona other than ourselves – has the effect of liberating an individual to explore the 'as if' realm (Heathcote 1984c, 104) of the 'subjunctive mood' (Turner 1982, 80, 82–83; 1990, 11–12). One consequence of working in-role is that participants are released from the pressure to 'get the right answer'. This is what she meant by the 'no penalty area' (1984e, 128–30) of in-role communication in which the participants experience the 'freedom to experiment without the burden of future repercussions' (1984c, 104) for this enables them to explore the worldview of others in ways that facilitate the possibility that new insights might emerge through in-role dialogues about ethical questions concerning the 'socio-historical context of relations' that lift awareness out of the classroom and situates the participants in a new relationship with one another and with the objects that mediate the learning encounter; what Heathcote calls 'the other' (1984f, 162–63). This focus upon 'the other' – as Heathcote's 'role conventions' or as Freire's 'compound codifications' – empowers us to collaboratively work with one another in a learning and teaching context that is substantially different from the normative relations that typify interactions between teachers and students when we do not assume fictive roles. For it is this new role-based perspective, in which we operate within a redefined 'no penalty area', that enables everyone to 'become capable of comparing, evaluating, intervening, deciding, taking new direction, and thereby constituting ourselves as ethical beings' (Freire 1998b, 38). This is especially the case when 'teacher in role' is used to provoke and empower both students and teachers to temporarily sidestep the power relationship that operates so strongly in transmission and inquiry classrooms – wherein all participants maintain their actual (real life) social roles as the standpoint from which they speak with one another in classroom communication events.

Implications for drama practice

I confess to a certain reticence in presuming to offer conclusions for my drama colleagues about the ideas presented here. Certainly, these learning and teaching propositions have informed and animated my own teaching practice for over three decades, and I suppose I feel that the conclusions, such as they might be concerning the utility of these concepts, are embedded within your contemplation of the schema offered in Table 7.1.

Yet as I examine these propositions in the light of concepts articulated by the NSW Department of Education and Communities' 'Quality Teaching in Drama' website (1999–2011) I find that Freire's and Heathcote's process advice and epistemic value statements to be entirely consistent with the perspectives presented concerning the 'intellectual', 'learning environment', and 'significance' statements[1] which characterise the 'dimensions of quality teaching'. When contrasted with the NSW Quality Teaching Model for developing units and assessment tasks, Paulo Freire's and Dorothy Heathcote's epistemological propositions provide very sturdy concepts with which to conduct a deeply theorised reflection on one's classroom learning and teaching practices.

---

1 (www.curriculumsupport.education.nsw.gov.au/digital_rev/leading_my_faculty/lo/pedagogy/Pedagogy_pop2.htm)

7 The drama of co-intentional dialogue

Drama teachers tend to be in the vanguard of progressive educational practice. Nevertheless, it should perhaps be said that the types of dialogical practice that both Dorothy Heathcote and Paulo Freire advocate not only takes more classroom time and requires us to closely monitor our approach to formulating problem-posing questions, but that this reorientation can present daunting challenges to both early-career teachers as well as to those who feel the accelerating pressure – from whatever source – to achieve high level examination results by their student cohorts. All teachers who are sincerely committed to achieving quality learning outcomes have high expectations and high hopes for the efficacy of their own teaching practice.

These propositions raise questions about how each of us might benefit from pausing to reassess our assumptions about our teaching practice; not only in terms of the NSW Quality Teaching Model but also in terms of how we value and apply concepts of 'co-intentional' dialogue and use 'role-shifted discourse' to resolve the 'teacher-student contradiction' in order to enlarge the student's 'power to tell' through the diverse ways in which our drama-based interactions with them puts the 'thought-language' of their 'life experience to use'. We take this approach because we are interested in expanding possibilities for inductive reasoning so that through their 'naming' of the world, they act to 'transform' it through depictive dramatic actions which engage them in reflexive dialogical reflections that have the capacity to generate new cognitive and affective understandings about what it means to be human.

Education is a site of cultural struggle; and the ways in which we join ourselves to the task of enlarging possibilities to dialogically express and co-intentionally embody our shared 'ontological vocation' of 'becoming more fully human' (Freire 1994b, 26, 73) will be defined by the ways in which we, as educators, act to enlarge the 'pedagogical space' (Freire 1998b, 64) in which both students and teachers are empowered to express ourselves as we use 'role-shifted discourse' to generate new understanding. The NSW Quality Teaching Model provides useful guidance for thinking about how we can act to create 'pedagogical space' that will facilitate strong learning outcomes for students through the engagement of drama-based practices that flow from either the new K–6 creative arts curriculum or the current Stages 4, 5, or 6 drama curricula in secondary school settings.

The state of the art

The discussion offered here proposes that the many different forms of 'role-shifted discourse' represent a dynamically creative form of 'cultural action' that is realised through the determination to democratise social relations by exploring the ways in which the *conscientização* process can expand opportunities for both students and teachers to develop a shared capacity for expressing creative agency as we engage one another in 'problem-posing', 'co-intentional' dialogue.

Works cited

Anderson LW & Sosniak LA (Eds) (1994). *Bloom's taxonomy: a forty-year retrospective*. Chicago: National Society for the Study of Education.
Barnett R (1997). *Higher education: a critical business*. Buckingham: Open University Press.
Bloom BS (1956-64). *Taxonomy of educational objectives: the classification of educational goals*. Vol. 1-2. London: Longmans.
Bolton G (1979). *Towards a theory of drama in education*. London: Longman.
Bolton G & Heathcote D (1999). *So you want to use role-play? A new approach in how to plan*. Stoke-on-Trent: Trentham Books.
Carroll J (1986a). Framing drama: some classroom strategies. *NADIE Journal*, 10(2): 5-7.
Carroll J (1986b). Taking the initiative: the role of drama in pupil/teacher talk. PhD Thesis. Newcastle-Upon-Tyne: University of Newcastle-Upon-Tyne.
Carroll J (1988). Terra incognita: mapping drama talk. *NADIE Journal*, 12(2): 13-22.
Carroll J (1980). *The treatment of Dr Lister*. Bathurst: Mitchell College of Advanced Education Press.
Collins D (1977). *Paulo Freire: his life, works and thought*. New York: Paulist Press.
Freire P (1973a). A few notions about the word 'conscientisation'. *Hard Cheese*, 1(1): 23-38.
Freire P (1972a). *Cultural action for freedom*. Harmondsworth: Penguin.
Freire P (1974). *Education for critical consciousness*. London: Sheed and Ward.
Freire P (1998a). *Education for critical consciousness*. New York: Continuum.
Freire P (1973b). Education, liberation and the church. *Study Encounter*, 9(1): 1-16.
Freire P (1996). *Letters to Cristina: reflections on my life and work*. New York: Routledge.
Freire P (1998b). *Pedagogy of freedom: ethics, democracy, and civic courage*. Lanham: Rowman & Littlefield Publishers.

Freire P (1972c). *Pedagogy of the oppressed*. Harmondsworth: Penguin.
Freire P (1994b). *Pedagogy of the oppressed*. Rev. edn. New York: Continuum.
Freire P & Macedo D (1987). *Literacy: reading the word & the world*. South Hadley: Bergin & Garvey.
Goffman E (1974). *Frame analysis: an essay on the organization of experience*. New York: Harper Torchbooks.
Guba EG (Ed.) (1990). *The paradigm dialog*. Newbury Park: SAGE Publications.
Heathcote D (1984a). Dorothy Heathcote's notes. In L Johnson & C O'Neill (Eds). *Dorothy Heathcote: collected writing on education and drama* (pp202–10). Evanston: Northwestern University Press.
Heathcote D (1984b). Drama as challenge. In L Johnson & C O'Neill (Eds). *Dorothy Heathcote: collected writing on education and drama* (pp80–89). Evanston: Northwestern University Press.
Heathcote D (1984c). From the particular to the universal. In L Johnson & C O'Neill (Eds). *Dorothy Heathcote: collected writing on education and drama* (pp103–10). Evanston: Northwestern University Press.
Heathcote D (1984d). Improvisation. In L Johnson & C O'Neill (Eds). *Dorothy Heathcote: collected writing on education and drama* (pp44–48). Evanston: Northwestern University Press.
Heathcote D (1984e). Material for significance. In L Johnson & C O'Neill (Eds). *Dorothy Heathcote: collected writing on education and drama* (pp126–37). Evanston: Northwestern University Press.
Heathcote D (1984f). Signs and portents. In L Johnson & C O'Neill (Eds). *Dorothy Heathcote: collected writing on education and drama* (pp160–69). Evanston: Northwestern University Press.
Little G (1983). *Report of the primary language survey 1980 and 1981*. Canberra: Canberra College of Advanced Education.
Morris R (Ed) (1970). *American heritage dictionary of the English language*. New York: Random House.
Neelands J & Goode T (2000). *Structuring drama work: a handbook of available forms in theatre and drama*. Cambridge: Cambridge University Press.
NSW Department of Education and Communities (1999–2011). *Quality teaching in drama: drama curriculum K–12* [Online]. Available: http://www.curriculumsupport.education.nsw.gov.au/secondary/creativearts/qualityteaching/drama/index.htm [Accessed 13 June 2013].
O'Neill C (1995). *Drama worlds: a framework for process drama*. Portsmouth: Heinemann.
O'Neill C & Lambert A (1982). *Drama structures: a practical handbook for teachers*. London: Hutchinson.
Schaffner M (1986). A matter of balance. *NADIE Journal*, 11(1): 15–19.

Shor I & Freire P (1987). *A pedagogy for liberation*. South Hadley: Bergin & Garvey.

Turner V (1990). Are there universals of performance in myth, ritual, and drama? In R Schechner & W Appel (Eds). *By means of performance* (pp8–18). Cambridge: Cambridge University Press.

Turner V (1982). *From ritual to theatre: the human seriousness of play*. New York: PAJ Publications.

8
Hold the phone: drama education and mobile technology

David Cameron and Rebecca Wotzko

> Precisely because it is technology that is always with us, and that is always on, the mobile telephone is potentially one of the most powerful transformative agents for drama and learning available so far (Carroll et al. 2006, 165).

In the six of years or so since 'the future is mobile' was proposed as one of the many possible futures of drama and education we have seen a revolution in the underlying consumer technologies that shaped that prediction. Take a moment to take stock of your personal gadgets and devices that might be loosely gathered under the term 'mobile media'. Smartphone? Media player? Tablet computer? Ebook reader? Soon we may have to include wearable computers such as the Google Glass head-mounted display (www.google.com/glass/start/) or Pebble smartwatches (getpebble.com). To help you, we've prepared a simple online checklist that you might like to complete before reading on:

http://www.surveymonkey.com/s/hold_the_phone

Australia is a country noted for embracing the latest in mobile phone technology. To use an ugly marketing term, smartphone 'pene-

---

Cameron D & Wotzko R (2015). Hold the phone: drama education and mobile technology. In M Anderson & C Roche (Eds). *The state of the art: teaching drama in the 21st century*, (149–169). Sydney: Sydney University Press.

tration' in Australia is at the second highest rate in the world behind Singapore, with 52 percent of the population over 16 years of age owning one of these latest generation handsets (Moses 2011). Penetration equates to popularity in the consumer market, but it particularly reflects the fact that many Australians have recently upgraded to these newer feature-rich smartphones, despite already owning a mobile phone. One can only imagine what these reports might show if younger people were included in the figures. In 2009 an estimated 841,000 Australian children, almost a third (31 percent) of all children in the nation, owned a mobile phone. Three-quarters (76 percent) of 12–14-year-olds owned a mobile phone (ABS 2012). At least one major study of media and communication technology in Australian family homes found no evident socio-economic barriers to mobile phone ownership, though at the time, advanced smartphone handsets were more common among city-based young people (ACMA 2008).

The same survey found that a number of other mobile products were finding their way into Australian family homes. For example, portable mp3/4 media players (76 percent) and handheld game consoles (48 percent) had a foothold in all households with young people, though the study found that there was tendency for more wealthy families to own the latest models of these devices. You may have already noted that this study pre-dated the introduction of the tablet computers that have now started to replace laptop and personal computers in many homes as we enter, what some describe as, a post-personal computer age. While these mobile devices may have smaller screens and constrained input options compared to personal computers, they offer a powerful and appealing combination of portability, constant connection to the internet and phone-like voice, text and video communication (Maximilien & Campos 2012, 2).

Schools, universities and workplaces are also now being tempted by a 'bring your own device' (BYOD) model of ICT services based on wireless access and cloud services to supplement or perhaps even replace centralised computer resources. The New Media Consortium's annual Horizon forecast for educational technology predicts the wider adoption of mobile devices, mobile applications (apps) and tablet computing for K–12 and higher education within the next year or less (Johnson et al. 2012). This recognises that mobile phones are a capable and pervasive technology, that mobile software apps are a simple and cheap –

or often free – way to add specific and personalised functionality to these devices, and that tablet computers rapidly build upon these features with a bigger screen and other tools to improve the overall casual computing experience.

This market penetration and the technical maturity of these devices do not of course translate smoothly into universal acceptance in the classroom. Some argue that these devices drive a new form of digital divide which will separate those who can use them to 'amplify' their learning experiences and those who are distracted by them (Halverson & Halverson 2012). A further divide exists at institutions between teachers who engage with these technologies and those that seek to restrict or block their presence.

Integrating with the lives of learners

This chapter suggests that drama is well placed to meet some of the challenges of mobile technology in the classroom, integrating students' and teachers' real-world enthusiasm for networked digital media with classroom-based drama. We recognise that there are a number of obstacles to the acceptance and adoption of these technologies within schools, and that some educators feel they should be 'locked and blocked' to reduce the associated disruptive or negative behaviours and practices. However, we also urge teachers and practitioners to engage with the growing volume of policies, guidelines and examples of using these devices and applications in supervised and engaging ways. A divide is emerging between those who use these tools as a teaching resource and those who ban them, and:

> there is a grave danger a group of young people, who are heavy users of such technology, will become even more disengaged with education, seeing it as irrelevant to the world they inhabit (Heppell & Chapman 2011, 2).

In their daily lives mobile technology enables young people to 'interact simultaneously with both the physical world and with digital information' (Facer et al. 2004), though it may be up to each individual in any given context as to whether this is focused interaction, or the mediated equivalent of daydreaming. There is also recognition that 'mobile devices have become one of the primary ways that youth interact with and learn from each other' (Johnson et al. 2012, 11), and this in turn contributes to the blurring of formal and informal educational settings and practices also noted in the *Horizon Report*.

It is always a challenge for both educators and students to navigate the inevitable slippages that are so common in the educational application of consumer technologies: informal versus formal use, private communication versus public collaboration, consumption versus production of content, and so on. We argue that this is an especially pressing issue when it comes to mobile technologies, primarily because of their pervasiveness; not just in terms of the numbers of devices we own, but in the ways that they are becoming a portal to many of our cultural, social and economic processes and activities. The proscriptive 'in the building, in the bag' approach to regulate use of these devices at school may soon be swept aside by wider adoption of the BYOD model, one that recognises how these devices can cut across many dimensions of students' lives in ways that sometimes render school boundaries or classroom walls irrelevant.

Clearly many of us – students, teachers, practitioners, audiences – are seduced en masse by these devices as consumers, but can we make a shift to more active creation of dramatic and educational content for and with these devices?

Get started with familiar dramatic conventions

One of the simplest and most fundamental strategies adopted by drama facilitators is to use 'particular conventions that can be quickly produced without the need for lengthy preparations or rehearsal' (Neelands 2004, 51). Existing dramatic conventions that are well tested and understood – or that at least can be found in many practical texts and primers – can therefore be modified to address or utilise the mobile media technologies that are common in our daily lives. Applying dramatic conventions to the information, communication and media channels commonly used by many participants in the drama makes the integration of those conventions seamless (Cameron 2009). Importantly, the use of conventions within a dramatic frame may in some cases negate the need to use the physical devices themselves, which could address some of the immediate concerns about their presence in some settings such as schools, hospitals or prisons.

Two powerful dramatic conventions to consider when working with media technologies in the classroom are those of framing and double framing. Drama can be used to create a cognitive and affective border to separate reality from the representation of reality that is the 'as if' world of the drama. Participants can thus be protected within a range of theatrical forms that enable them to work with greater conviction, where the role-based activities distance them from unstructured and naturalistic work that may be too close to real life for comfort, or to sustain belief (Carroll 1986). Double framing occurs when 'one dramatic perspective into the event has been placed within another to provide a double layer of protection and distance', for example as with the Everyday Theatre project (O'Connor et al. 2006, 239). In this applied theatre project the students are framed as helping a fictional family deal with issues of family life and thus do not have to talk about their own families; furthermore this occurs within the additional frame of playing a video game.

Drama educators and practitioners familiar with working with framing and other drama conventions are therefore well equipped with techniques that can be used to explore and address concerns about inappropriate behaviours associated with young people and emerging technology, because:

> by providing role protection and role distance through drama and physical theatre, teachers can help provide the emotional literacy required for their students in a way that is not catered for in other areas of curriculum (Carroll et al. 2006, 35).

Further examples of how to 'mashup' drama conventions to accommodate contemporary digital, mobile and online technology already exist elsewhere (Cameron 2009; Carroll & Cameron 2009), but here we will focus on a small sample to illustrate how they might be refreshed and used in classroom drama to acknowledge and explore the ubiquitous presence of mobile media technology and cultures. They are drawn from the descriptions collated in *Structuring drama work* (Neelands & Goode 2000) and *Beginning drama 11–14* (Neelands 2004). Page references for these sources are cited with each basic description, along with commentary on the adaptations made possible by mobile media forms.

'Overheard conversations'

The participants overhear a conversation, allowing for new information or tension to be introduced (Neelands 2004, 103; Neelands & Goode 2000, 37). This convention sits well with the dramatic tensions made possible by the use of mobile telephones in public spaces, where it might be difficult to avoid hearing one side of a 'private' conversation. Text-based forms of conversations such as Short Message Service (SMS) messages or instant messaging might also fall into this category, and can be 'overheard' (read) by gaining accidental or deliberate access to someone else's device.

SMS is synonymous with the act of 'texting'. SMS messages were originally limited to 160 characters (including spaces). The preferred form of mobile communication for young people is SMS, which has evolved a language and subculture of its own. Goggin notes that there 'has been much fascination in studying, cataloguing, and debating the varieties and intricacies of text messaging, and how it has modified social, media, and cultural practices' (2006, 65). And messaging is now a means by which young Australians initiate, maintain and dissolve intimate relationships with each other (ACMA 2007, 293).

'Diaries, letters, journals, messages'

The facilitator delivers information to the whole group or a subgroup to introduce new ideas, information or tension; or participants can write them in or out of character (Neelands 2004, 102; Neelands & Goode 2000, 16). The forms of personal publication made possible through mobile devices can be adopted for this convention including: SMS messages, email, Facebook posts or comments, discussion board comments, Twitter 'tweets', Instagram photos, or instant messages. Mobile devices are a portal to most web-based publishing systems, particularly through specialist software apps, therefore the list of forms that could be adopted for this convention is seemingly endless, and can be updated as new services appear. Tablet and ebook readers, with their larger screens, might be used to read lengthier documents rendered in electronic form.

Instant messaging (IM) is a form of communication in which users 'chat' through short text messages, often in real-time or in a form resembling a conversation, though some types can be used in a similar way to email. In some services the messages may also include small graphical 'emoticons' and other media elements. IM can take place person-to-person or in virtual spaces known generically as 'chat rooms', and although replaced to some extent by social media updates it is still heavily used by young people in preference to other forms such as email (Lenhart et al. 2005). Video and audio chat tools also exist.

'Making maps/diagrams'

Participants make maps or diagrams within the drama to reflect on experience or to aid problem solving (Neelands & Goode 2000, 19). Many mobile devices now include GPS or similar functionality which can be used by participants to incorporate real geospatial data (e.g. latitude, longitude, altitude) into the drama. Social media services such as Facebook, Twitter and Foursquare allow for users to 'check-in' in order to indicate their presence at a physical location at a certain time. Geotagging technology also allows for geographical data to be attached to images. GPS-equipped devices can often download maps of areas to be incorporated into the drama. The potential use of the mapping and locative functions of these mobile devices is evident in fully realised drama and game projects such as C&T's *Stratar* (2012) and Blast Theory's *Uncle Roy all around you* (2003).

'Objects of character' (or 'private property')

A character is introduced or fleshed-out through the consideration of carefully chosen personal belongings. The objects can be 'found' at any point in the drama, and can even suggest a contradictory subtext to their behaviour (Neelands 2004, 103; Neelands & Goode 2000, 20). The private property left behind can obviously include a device itself. The amount of personal information and customised content to be found on these devices makes it possible to provide rich clues on a character or situation, using a variety of media forms. Losing one of these devices, especially one carrying important and sensitive personal information, can highlight the traces of identity or 'character' we transfer and store in them through general use.

'Soundtracking' (also 'Soundscape')

Sounds are used to accompany or describe an environment, to create a mood, and can perhaps be taken from one situation to illustrate another. Sounds can be natural or stylised, live or pre-recorded, and can include dialogue and musical instruments. (Neelands 2004, 73; Neelands & Goode 2000, 24). Many of these devices have the capacity to play sound files either as ringtones, alerts or as a media player function. Portable media players can be connected to sound systems to be played to a group. Apps to simulate musical instruments and to compose, record and edit music and sound files are freely available for many devices, as are audio note-taking and text-to-speech functions.

'Collective character'

A character is improvised by the group, with any participant able to speak as the character. There is no need for conformity in the responses participants have, and differences of opinion or attitude allow for group discussion about the character (Neelands 2004, 101). Many video and online games incorporate a stage or process of creating an online character to represent each participant (known as an avatar). This is particularly the case in 3D graphic spaces, where the construction of the avatar can involve a 'paper doll' style process of selecting attributes such as physical appearance and clothing. The creation of personal profiles in online publishing and social networking sites is also a process similar to character creation, in which personal details, physical attributes, and likes and dislikes can be shared with others. Mobile devices that can access these apps, games or online sites might make use of this convention.

'Unfinished materials'

An object provides a clue or partial information as a starting point for the drama (Neelands 2004, 104; Neelands & Goode 2000, 28). Collaborative publishing tools such as wikis are accessible through many mobile devices, with participants invited to edit and complete an unfinished article. The 'edit history' and 'discussion' features used by wikis to track changes can be brought into play here as clues to the origin of the materials. Video, audio and photographic materials can be made available online through content sharing sites, with the comment and tagging functions used by participants to discuss the material and build upon it with their own contributions. File-sharing and online cloud storage sites might be used as a repository for mysterious digital files containing unfinished work.

Become a 'maker' – using mobile devices for production

In addition to generating or refreshing dramatic conventions to accommodate contemporary mobile technology, a further opportunity remains to use these devices as production tools. Smartphones, tablets and even some media players and game consoles come equipped with the tools and functions that enable them to be used as multimedia production platforms. Cameras that enable still and video recording or even live streaming are a standard feature on these devices, so much so, that issues of privacy and appropriate behaviour abound. Nonetheless, like all tools, when used appropriately and with due attention to risk, the creative outcomes can be worthwhile.

Drama educators and practitioners are using digital storytelling in both school and informal settings to examine young peoples' expressions of self and identity depicted through combinations of performance and creative practice in multimodal digital platforms (Wales 2012). Exploring this blend of oral storytelling, digital media and performance (Chung 2007) through mobile media seems a relevant and practical variation of the method. More broadly, the evolution of digital and online technology has encouraged participatory cultures access to young people where 'fans and other consumers are invited to actively participate in the creation and circulation of new media content' (Jenkins 2008, 331). Engagement with this participatory culture allows the audience to move on a sliding scale from consumer to producer of media content, or 'produser' (Bruns 2008), much like how drama encourages the move from audience to participant or 'spectactor' (Boal 1995).

There is commonly a low technical barrier to contributing and participating in the creation and publication activities afforded by this technology. That's good news for teachers and practitioners who may not have the time, or inclination, to learn or teach advanced technical procedures as a prelude to the creative activity itself. However, these forms may require teachers to recognise new sets of cultural competencies and skills such as: play, performance, simulation, appropriation, multitasking, distributed cognition, collective intelligence, judgement, transmedia navigation, networking and negotiation (Jenkins et al. 2009, 4).

These are areas that many might already engage with in classroom-based drama, mediated performances and digital storytelling, but which are understood under different terminology or in different contexts. All imply a hands-on or active approach to learning when linked with the concept of a participatory educational culture enabled by technology. In this section we survey some of the functionality and affordances of mobile media devices and related technology that might be incorporated into production-based methods of drama and education. There are rich opportunities here for drama educators and practitioners to draw upon smaller elements of the available technologies that might be used as a focus for a creative production activity, or as a means of publishing and sharing some of the creative artefacts generated through interactions of performance and media technology.

Media content production and sharing sites

Video and image sharing services are examples of sites and activities formed around digital content production and sharing. These services typically provide the storage space and bandwidth, and aggregate the content into a searchable database. Content on these sites might be rated or ranked according to user votes or popularity. Some services also allow viewers to contribute text-based comments, or to link their own video responses to an entry in the same way that some text-based forms, such as forums, will thread related comments. Examples include YouTube (www.youtube.com) and Vimeo (www.vimeo.com).

Similar to video sharing services, there are internet applications to allow the sharing of digital image content via online photographic galleries. Some services allow users to control access to galleries, deeming them for private or public viewing. Users may be encouraged to post comments, or to rate and rank images or galleries. The use of user-generated keywords to identify photographic content is increasing, and copyright controls are an issue, as digital images can easily be copied from the web. Privacy is also a growing concern, particularly as images may be published directly from mobile phone cameras. There are now many mobile apps that streamline the process of taking, editing, manipulating, uploading and sharing images from the device itself – with the end result made available either through specialised online image repositories like Flickr (www.flickr.com), or more directly via personal profiles on social media and other publishing sites. Image-based social media services such as Instagram (www.instagram.com) and Snapchat (www.snapchat.com) are popular with young people, fuelled by the ubiquitous nature of mobile devices.

QR codes

Designed for manufacturing processes and adopted for marketing purposes, these codes are becoming a more common way to direct mobile device users to a web resource. A Quick Response code (QR code) is a variation on barcode principles for machine-readable data that contains dots arranged within a square. Users can access the information contained within the code using a QR reader or scanner app that makes use of the camera on a mobile device. Some phones include a native QR reader, whereas others require download of a third party application. Information encoded within the QR code can often include a web address; the example given in Figure 8.1 was generated with a free online service, and links to the web-based survey created for readers of this chapter.

The state of the art

Figure 8.1 A QR code containing a link to a web page

Augmented reality

This is a form of mediated experience that combines or augments live views of a real-world environment with computer-generated input such as data, video, images or audio. Augmented reality systems are being used to develop a variety of entertainment, educational, scientific and professional applications. Mobile media devices equipped with still or video camera capability are being used for this type of experience; one recent example is the Powerhouse Museum Layar application that creates a historical tour of Sydney (www.powerhousemuseum.com/layar/). The software services and apps to generate this content are becoming more within the reach of the casual or novice user, with some using QR code technology to trigger or position the data being displayed over the camera image.

Geotagging

Many mobile devices now incorporate a Global Positioning System (GPS) function, which enables the user to plot their location via the GPS satellite network. Geotagging is the process of adding this geographical data (e.g. latitude and longitude) to other media types such as images or QR codes. For example, combining a camera phone with

8 Hold the phone: drama education and mobile technology

GPS allows the user to take photos that include embedded information about the location at which the picture was taken. Geotagging data usually consists of latitude and longitude coordinates, though it may also contain information such as altitude, bearing, distance and place names.

Wikis, social bookmarking, tagging

Wiki software (named after a Hawaiian word for 'fast') enables users to add, remove, and edit content of a website. The collaborative encyclopaedia, Wikipedia, is one of the best-known examples. Bookmarks were developed as a way to store, organise, share and manage lists of links to online resources such as websites. Web browsing software includes this feature to enable individuals to return to sites without having to remember complex web addresses. The concept of social bookmarking extends this into web-based sharable lists, often built around topics or themes; examples include Delicious (www.delicious.com) and Diigo (www.diigo.com). The use of keywords or tags creates searchable user-generated classifications for bookmarks. The use of keywords or tags is a way of building a description of a digital object by allowing users and viewers to contribute to the definition. There are many applications that allow staff and students to create, share and access information with these types of services via mobile devices.

Ringtones, sounds and music

A ringtone is of course the sound made by a mobile phone to indicate an incoming call or message. Many handsets are now capable of playing audio files in the same digital formats used by portable media players, so ringtones can be high quality reproductions of popular songs or other sound effects. The production and sale of ringtones is an industry in its own right, and software exists to allow users to record and create their own ringtones for some handsets. The use of sound cues is common for a range of functions across a suite of mobile devices.

Many mobile devices such as smartphones, tablets and some media players are equipped with basic audio input (microphone) and output (headset) functions. There are also specialist manufacturers who have produced hardware connectors to integrate these devices with amplified audio systems, computer-based music composing systems, high-quality microphones, and for use as controllers or signal processors for musical instruments such as electronic keyboard and guitars. There are apps that turn the devices themselves into synthesised music instruments for live performance, or to provide music composing and recording functions.

Many mobile devices can also be used as media players to playback sounds, audio files, and even live radio through internet streaming or built-in FM radio receivers.

Social networking sites

Online communities formed around common interests have long been a feature of the internet, and many of the services now extend into the mobile media space by allowing content editing and updating via mobile phones. The software tools to enable people to connect with each other and to easily share content in variety of forms have developed into a set of applications known generally as social networking services.

These sites generally allow a user to create a unique online personal profile, which forms an identity that can be shared with other users. Links have been made between these accounts, so that content and information can be shared. Most allow for different levels of private and public content sharing. These sites also contain tools to allow a high degree of personalisation, ranging from image galleries, blogs and messaging tools, polls, games, quizzes, status updates, calendars, event coordination, and collaborative groups. These features lend themselves to a variety of ways in which drama participants can engage with characters through commenting, messaging, sharing links and discussing content (Wotzko & Carroll 2009).

Blogs, micro-blogs, podcasting

A blog (web log) is a journal-style online publication that typically displays the newest entries first. Blogs tend to be written by one person, though 'blogging' is being adopted as an online publication form for non-personal uses such as journalism, public relations and political campaigning. Key features of blogs are links to other online resources (especially other blogs) and the ability for readers to add comments to

8 Hold the phone: drama education and mobile technology

individual entries. Blogging software is a content management system (CMS) that generally makes the process of publishing content online easier for people with limited web publishing skills. Mobile blogging or moblogging is the publishing of blog entries directly to the web from a mobile device. Photographs taken with a camera phone are a popular form of moblog content, as many phones now allow images to be sent directly to a website for publication. Text-based moblog entries tend to be quite short, due to the awkwardness of many mobile phone keypads.

While blogs can contain multimedia such as images and videos as well as text, an expressly video-based form of blogging is sometimes described as a vlog (video log). Podcasting uses similar underlying technologies to blogging, but is based around the syndication and downloading of audio files. Vodcasting is a term used to describe a similar use of video content.

Micro-blogging is a form in which users write particularly brief text updates – 140 characters maximum in the case of Twitter – often providing pithy observations, or a running narrative of events. Status updates on social networking services such as Facebook provide a similar function. Micro-blogging is increasingly finding journalistic, marketing and public affairs applications, and the possibilities for drama and role-play are emerging (Wotzko 2012). Posts can contain links to other media such as images, longer articles, or video. A culture of monitoring real-time themes (trending) has emerged around micro-blogging.

Portable passions: using mobile devices to engage with affinity spaces

So far we have offered ways in which mobile media might be considered and applied within the existing educational and dramatic structures familiar to teachers and practitioners. We've also surveyed some of the affordances of mobile and related technology that might be used to generate or publish media products during the course of drama activities taking place within formal settings. Now we move into less familiar territory, but one which offers hope of productive engagement with young people in the myriad informal learning spaces made possible by networked digital media.

The concept of the 'affinity space' (Gee 2004) is gaining currency among those interested in the literary, learning and production practices occurring within the spaces linked to the passionate interests of young people. Affinity spaces are the physical and virtual spaces (or a blend of the two) where young people come together around a shared interest. Examples can be found in the online fan communities formed around popular culture interests such *The Sims* video games, *The Hunger Games* novels, and the *Neopets* online game (Lammers et al. 2012). Gee's original description was of a single portal, though it is now recognised that affinity spaces might make use of a range of media production and social sharing sites that link in and out of an online portal such as a discussion board. Some of the features of these contemporary affinity spaces are:

- having a common endeavour is primary
- participation is self-directed, multifaceted and dynamic
- participation and production of creative content is often multimodal in online spaces
- they afford a passionate, public audience for content
- socialising plays an important part in participation
- leadership roles vary within and among spaces
- knowledge is distributed across the space
- many place a high value on cataloguing and documenting content and practices
- they encompass a variety of media-specific and social networking portals (Lammers et al. 2012, 48–50).

The focus on the space(s) where passionate interests are turned into a shared endeavour, rather than the group or community itself, is an important distinction. The research interest in affinity spaces is, in part, a response to the perceived limitations of other frameworks for examining social learning and notably, communities of practice, where groups of people 'share a concern or a passion for something they do and learn how to do it better as they interact regularly' (Wenger 1998, 1). An immediate problem arises as to who belongs to the community and who doesn't, which focuses attention on membership. This is not surprising given that creators of the communities of practice framework argued that 'identity, knowing and social membership entail one another' (Lave & Wenger 1991, 53). However, as DeVane argues, the loosely knit social relations in schools and workplaces often challenge conventional interpretations of 'community', and the 'anonymous and ephemeral social ties commonly found on internet sites render it nearly incoherent' (2012, 165).

As we have already noted, mobile media devices are not only a platform for communication, collaboration and the consumption and production of content in their own right; they are also a means by which many people make use of online media and social networking portals to pursue their passions. The rising popularity of social curation applications with simple but powerful mobile interfaces such as: Pinterest (www.pinterest.com), Storify (www.storify.com), Flipboard (www.flipboard.com) and Tumblr (www.tumblr.com), reflect increasing engagement in affinity spaces from mobile platforms. As with communities of practice, it is tempting to consider ways in which to harness these affinity spaces in the service of formal educational structures. However, Duncan and Hayes argue for:

> a 'middle path', considering digital media and online interactions not for how we should manage them or necessarily accommodate them within existing educational structures, but for what they tell us about the forms of learning and literacy that are already instantiated within the use of these media. (2012 p. 3)

We make a distinction between mobile devices and general cultural practices around mobile media, and the affinity spaces that can be accessed from a range of mobile media.

Conclusion

Throughout this chapter we have attempted to give drama educators and practitioners some starting points from which to consider the practical implications of working with emerging mobile media conventions and the affordances of mobile technology. Rapidly evolving smartphone and tablet devices are becoming universal machines, replacing what until quite recently would have been separate devices like cameras, media players and games consoles. Their utility can be expanded and upgraded easily by downloading small pieces of software. These devices are becoming ubiquitous and pervasive in our lives, and this trend is becoming more evident with new wearable technology appearing in forms based on eyeglasses and wristwatches.

Institutions are increasingly recognising the presence of these devices in their planning around infrastructure, policies and practices for ICT support. Educators are already faced with some of the issues that arise, for example whether these devices are distractions from, or amplifiers of, learning, and in which contexts they might connect with formal learning settings. This chapter suggests that drama is well placed to meet some of the challenges of mobile technology in the classroom, integrating students' and teachers' real-world enthusiasm for networked digital media with classroom-based drama.

We do balance this by urging caution when working in the increasingly blurred boundaries of formal and informal learning spaces. Attempts to remake classrooms into affinity spaces, or co-opt affinity spaces into the educational system, would risk losing the very factors that make these spaces an appealing model for learning. Rather, we encourage drama educators to help young people develop the skills and competencies for engaging with new media proposed by Jenkins and others, so that they are better equipped to learn and contribute creatively in the affinity spaces formed around the things that matter to them. To prohibit or ignore mobile media in formal educational settings gives greater weight to their ability to distract learners rather than to amplify learning. This may also diminish drama's ability to give us a 'heightened opportunity' (Stern 2008, 114) to engage with young peoples' cultural and identity production activities (Nafus & Tracey 2002), based around the media forms and devices now forming a key part of youth culture (Downie & Glazebrook 2007; Goggin 2006).

Students are finding creative opportunities through these technologies to pursue their personal passions through making and sharing. At the same time there are renewed opportunities to expand the role of teachers and practitioners as pedagogical innovators. An ongoing challenge is to develop and share ways of teaching through these technologies in ways that leverage the emerging affordances and cultural practices, while remaining focused on the real lives of the participants.

Works cited

Australian Bureau of Statistics (ABS). (2012). *Children's participation in cultural and leisure activities*, Australia, April 2012, cat. no. 4901.0 [Online]. Available: http://www.abs.gov.au/ausstats/abs@.nsf/mf/4901.0 [Accessed 15 December 2013].

Australian Communications and Media Authority (ACMA) (2007). *Media and communications in Australian families 2007: report of the media and society research project*. Canberra: Australian Communications & Media Authority.

Australian Communications and Media Authority (ACMA) (2008). Access to the internet, broadband and mobile phones in family households *Media and communications in Australian families* (Vol. 3, pp. 1–17).

Blast Theory (2003). *Uncle Roy all around you* [Online]. Available: http://www.blasttheory.co.uk/bt/work_uncleroy.html [Accessed 15 December 2013].

Boal A (1995). *The rainbow of desire*. London: Routledge.

Bruns A (2008). *Blogs, Wikipedia, Second life, and beyond: from production to produsage*. New York: Peter Lang Publishing.

C&T (2012). *Stratar* [Online]. Available: http://www.candt.org/applications/stratar [Accessed 15 December 2013].

Cameron D (2009). Mashup: digital media and drama conventions. In M Anderson, J Carroll & D Cameron (Eds). *Drama education with digital technology* (pp52–66). London: Continuum.

Carroll J (1986). *Framing drama: some classroom strategies*. National Association for Drama in Education Journal, 12(2).

Carroll J, Anderson M & Cameron D (2006). *Real players? Drama, technology and education*. Staffordshire: Trentham.

Carroll J & Cameron D (2009). Drama, digital pre-text, and social media. *Research in Drama Education: The Journal of Applied Theatre and Performance*, 14(2): 295–312.

Chung SK (2007). Art education technology: digital storytelling. *Art Education*, 60(2): 17–22.

DeVane B (2012). Whither membership? Identity and social learning in affinity spaces. In ER Hayes & SC Duncan (Eds), *Learning in video game affinity spaces* (pp162–85). New York: Peter Lang Publishing.

Downie C & Glazebrook K (2007). Mobile phones and the consumer kids: Research Paper 41: *the Australia institute*.

Duncan SC & Hayes ER (2012). Expanding the affinity space: an introduction. In ER Hayes & SC Duncan (Eds). *Learning in video game affinity spaces* (pp1–22). New York: Peter Lang Publishing.

Facer K, Joiner R, Stanton D, Reid J, Hull R & Kirk D (2004). Savannah: mobile gaming and learning? *Journal of Computer Assisted Learning*, 20(6): 399–409. doi: 10.1111/j.1365-2729.2004.00105.x

Gee JP (2004). *Situated language and learning: a critique of traditional schooling.* New York: Routledge.

Goggin G (2006). *Cell phone culture*. London: Routledge.

Halverson ER & Halverson R (2012). *The design and assessment of 21st century learning environments*. Recorded presentation, Centre for Research on Computer Supported Learning and Cognition, The University of Sydney [Online]. Available: http://webconf.ucc.usyd.edu.au/p7ek82a56rw/ [Accessed 15 December 2013].

Heppell S & Chapman C (2011). Effective practice for schools moving to end locking and blocking in the classroom *Cloudlearn project* [Online]. Available: http://rubble.heppell.net/cloudlearn/media/Cloudlearn_Report.pdf [Accessed 15 December 2013].

Jenkins H (2008). *Convergence culture: where old and new media collide*. New York: New York University Press.

Jenkins H, Clinton K, Purushotma R, Robison AJ & Weigel M (2009). *Confronting the challenges of participatory culture: media education for the 21st Century*. Chicago: The Macarthur Foundation.

Johnson L, Adams S & Cummins M (2012). *NMC horizon report: 2012 K–12 edition*. Austin: The New Media Consortium.

Lammers JC, Curwood JS & Magnifico AM (2012). Toward an affinity space methodology: considerations for literacy research. *English Teaching: Practice and Critique*, 11(2): 44–58.

Lave J & Wenger E (1991). *Situated learning: legitimate peripheral participation*. Cambridge: Cambridge University Press.

Lenhart A, Madden M & Hitlin P (2005). Teens and technology, *Pew internet and American life project* [Online] Available: http://www.pewinternet.org/2005/07/27/teens-and-technology/

Maximilien EM & Campos P (2012). Facts, trends and challenges in modern software development. *International Journal of Agile and Extreme Software Development*, 1(1): 1–5.

Moses A (2011, 8 September). Australia's white hot smartphone revolution, *Sydney Morning Herald* [Online]. Available: http://www.smh.com.au/digital-life/mobiles/australias-white-hot-smartphone-revolution-20110908-1jz3k.html [Accessed 15 December 2013].

Nafus D & Tracey K (2002). Mobile phone consumption and concepts of personhood. In J Katz & M Aakhus (Eds). *Perpetual contact: mobile communication, private talk, public performance*. Cambridge: Cambridge University Press.

Neelands J (2004). *Beginning drama 11-14*. 2nd edn. London: David Fulton Publishers.

Neelands J & Goode T (2000). *Structuring drama work: a handbook of available forms in theatre and drama*. 2nd edn. Cambridge: Cambridge University Press.

O'Connor P, O'Connor B & Welsh-Morris M (2006). Making the everyday extraordinary: a theatre in education project to prevent child abuse, neglect and family violence. *Research in drama education: The journal of Applied Theatre and Performance*, １1(2): 235-45.

Stern S (2008). Producing sites, exploring identities: youth online authorship. In D Buckingham (Ed). *Youth, identity and digital media*. Cambridge, MA: MIT Press.

Wales P (2012). Telling tales in and out of school: youth performativities with digital storytelling. *Research in Drama Education: The Journal of Applied Theatre and Performance*, 17(4): pp535-52.

Wenger E (1998). *Communities of practice: learning, meaning and identity*. Cambridge: Cambridge University Press.

Wotzko R (2012). Newspaper Twitter: applied drama and microblogging. *Research in Drama Education: The Journal of Applied Theatre and Performance*, 17(4): 569-81.

Wotzko R & Carroll J (2009). Digital theatre and online narrative. In M Anderson, J Carroll & D Cameron (Eds), *Drama education with digital technology*. London: Continuum.

About the contributors

Jerry Boland is senior lecturer at the School of Communication and Creative Industries at the Charles Sturt University, Bathurst, NSW. A recipient of an Australian Learning & Teaching Council (ALTC) citation for teaching excellence in 2007 and 2010, he is a Research Fellow of the CSU Education for Practice Institute (EFPI). Jerry has worked as an educator, performer, and director in a variety of Australian and overseas environments. He studied mime, mask and physical comedy with master teachers Carlo Mazzone-Clementi and Jon Paul Cook at the Dell'Arte International School of Physical Theatre in Blue Lake, California; wood sculpting/leather mask fabrication; commedia dell'arte performance with Antonio Fava in Reggio nell' Emilia, Italy; and drama in education with Dorothy Heathcote at the University of Newcastle-Upon-Tyne.

David Cameron is deputy director of Academic Technologies at the University of Newcastle. David's research interests include digital game-based learning, the use of 'everyday' networked media technologies in learning and teaching, and the application of applied drama conventions and techniques to produce engaging blended learning activities. David is co-author of *Real players?* (2006) and co-editor of *Drama education with digital technologies* (2009) with Michael Anderson and the late, and still greatly missed, John Carroll. David has a professional and teaching background in media and communication, including radio journalism and community broadcasting.

Victoria Campbell has been a drama educator, storyteller and performer for more than 20 years. She is passionate about the role of the arts, particularly drama in the lives of young people. Her interest in oral storytelling and narrative performance lead to sustained research in this area resulting in the completion of both a MEd (2008) and PhD (2013) at the University of Sydney. Victoria's doctoral thesis explored the implications of four early-career primary teachers, creating a narrative performance based on their experiences of teaching. She is currently a lecturer in drama (K–6) at the University of Sydney. For the past four years she has been a teaching artist for the Sydney Theatre Company's School Drama program.

Robyn Ewing is professor of teacher education and the arts, and Acting ProDean, Faculty of Education and Social Work at the University of Sydney. Robyn's teaching, research and extensive publications include a focus on the use of drama strategies with literature to enhance primary students' English and literacy learning and she is currently working in partnership with Sydney Theatre Company on the School Drama project. She is national resident of the Australian Literacy Educators Association, vice-president of the Sydney Story Factory Board and a member of the Australian Film, Television and Radio School (AFTRS) Council. Robyn is a recipient of the Lady Cutler Award for distinguished service to children's literature (2012) and was recently made a fellow of the Australian College of Educators.

Paul Gardiner is an experienced drama and English teacher, having taught in secondary schools for 17 years. He is currently one of the senior markers for the scriptwriting component of the NSW HSC Drama examination and is a member of the HSC Drama exam committee. Paul has also written a number of plays, two of which have been shortlisted for Playwriting Australia's National Script workshop. He currently teaches in the areas of teacher education and theatre learning, and is conducting research into playwriting pedagogy in secondary schools, creativity theory and the teacher-student dynamic.

About the contributors

Robyn Gibson has been a primary-school teacher, art/craft specialist and tertiary educator in Australia and the United States. Her research has focused on children's attitudes to art, art making and art education, and primary-school education in the visual and creative arts. She co-authored (with Robyn Ewing) *Transforming the curriculum through the arts* (2011). And she is currently engaged as the evaluator of School Drama with the Sydney Theatre Company. Beyond the university, she chairs the Australian Film, Television and Radio School's (AFTRS) Schools Advisory Committee.

Robyn is an advocate for the imperative of creativity within the curriculum and has been nominated for the Faculty's Excellence in Teaching Award six times, including in 2007, when she won.

Christine Hatton is a lecturer and researcher in the areas of drama, curriculum, creative arts education and technology. She is a past president of Drama NSW and has served as Director of Research for Drama Australia. She was the last state Drama Curriculum Advisor K–12 for the NSW Department of Education and Training. She has worked with pre-service drama and primary teachers in Sydney, Edinburgh, Singapore and Townsville. Her research and publications have explored the intersections of gender, narrative and identity in the drama classroom, with a particular focus on the learning and teaching of adolescent girls. She co-authored (with Sarah Lovesy) *Young at art: classroom playbuilding in practice* (2009) and regularly leads professional development workshops for teachers and artists.

Margery Hertzberg lectured at the University of Western Sydney's School of Education for 20 years and is currently an independent drama, English, language and literacy consultant and researcher. She is especially committed to working with students from socio-economically disadvantaged communities. Her key research interest concerns how drama can enhance children's English, language and literacy development – particularly students learning English as an additional language. She is former president of PETAA and a current board member of ATESOL, NSW. She presents regularly at National and International conferences and has published widely. Her most recent book, *Teaching English language learners in mainstream classes* (2012), explains why drama methodology enhances English language learners' literacy, English and language development.

Helen Hristofski has extensive knowledge and experience in Australia's youth theatre and arts education sector. Helen studied at the Western Australian Academy of Performing Arts, has degrees in education and arts management, and is an honorary associate of the University of Sydney. Helen was the education manager at Bell Shakespeare, worked as a coordinator for Performing Lines, and is currently the education manager at Sydney Theatre Company. Helen has worked to co-produce, present and commission the work of many small-to-medium-sized companies over the years. She was a pioneer for digital live streaming of performances particularly to remote locations. Helen has a keen interest in offering theatre programs in regional areas to provide opportunities that are relevant to communities, and work to build their capacity, resilience and cohesiveness.

Miranda Jefferson is an education consultant with the Captivate program in arts pedagogy, literacy and teacher professional learning for the Catholic Education Office Parramatta Diocese. She teaches drama, media arts learning and teacher professional practice in the Education and Social Work Faculty at the University of Sydney. Miranda co-authored *Teaching the screen: film education for generation next* (2009) and has contributed chapters to *Drama education with digital technology* (2009), *Imagination, innovation and creativity* (2009) and *Teenagers and reading* (2012). She is on the Arts Curriculum advisory board for the Australian Curriculum, Assessment and Reporting Authority, Chief Examiner Drama for the NSW Board of Studies and Vice-President of Australian Teachers of Media NSW. Miranda received an outstanding professional service award for drama education in 2008.

Sarah Lovesy is a freelance drama education consultant implementing a wide range of workshops for drama students and teachers around Australia. She also provides consulting advice to schools who wish to remodel and transform their drama departments or CAPA faculties to provide dynamic drama and creative arts learning for the 21st century. She is a casual lecturer and tutor at the universities of Western Sydney and Wollongong, teaching students to become drama teachers. Sarah has been actively involved with the New South Wales Board of Studies Junior and Senior Drama Syllabus Committees and their respective writing teams, as well as writing for various journals and educational bodies. She co-authored (with Christine Hatton) *Young at art: classroom playbuilding in practice* (2009).

Rebecca Wotzko teaches and researches in the School of Communication and Creative Industries at Charles Sturt University in Bathurst, NSW. Research interests include participatory culture, digital games, and the intersection between live and mediated performance. Her recent publications have explored combining social media and applied drama, and the intersection of digital games and drama. Rebecca is currently studying for her PhD on the convergent area of applied drama and digital technology.

David Wright is senior lecturer and director of higher degree research at the School of Education in the University of Western Sydney. He entered UWS as a lecturer in drama method and has since worked in programs in social ecology and contemporary performance. He currently works with undergraduate and postgraduate coursework students in units in social ecology and transformative learning, in all of which he draws on and applies the body-based learning that is central to drama practice. David has published widely in edited collections and academic journals. His work traverses embodied learning; arts-based research, constructivism and systems theory, imaginative education, cross-cultural learning and ecological understanding. David has also written for stage, film and television and has published works of creative fiction. He recently edited the book (with Catherine Camden-Pratt and Stuart Hill) *Social ecology: applying ecological understanding to our lives and our planet* (2011) and is increasingly interested in how drama-styled learning can be applied to the facilitation of a deeper understanding of the relationships that sustain community, in the context of significant challenges to ecological balance.

Index

ability 77, 91, 102, 120
adaptability 69
affinity space 164
anxiety 117, 119
assumptions 50, 63, 130, 145
audience engagement 12, 57, 62, 76, 80, 124
awareness 63, 64, 98, 118, 143

Carroll, John 132
character 3, 10, 39, 62, 76, 111, 116, 156
   objects of character 155
children's literature 26
   literary texts 26, 30
   picture books 12, 16, 18, 30, 94, 97
   spaces to play 97
classroom practice 30, 68, 72, 73, 79, 113, 144, 151
cloze strategy 88
collaborative learning 9, 14, 69, 81
collective experience 56, 63
compliance culture 14, 86
conflict in drama 49, 51
consciousness 50, 60, 62, 140
control 72, 91, 102, 118

creativity 16, 68, 74, 79, 116, 118, 121, 139
critical being 132
critical thinking 11, 16, 69, 77
Csikszentmihalyi, Mihaly 118, 122
cultural action 130, 141
cultural literacies 135
curriculum 4, 6, 26, 67
   change and development x, 6, 14, 131
   NSW curriculum 3, 67, 80
   primary curriculum 26
   secondary curriculum 11

deeper learning 15, 19, 96, 100
   abstract thinking 87
   interpersonal skills 19, 79
   intrapersonal skills 19
drama framework 43, 73, 131, 134, 138
drama literacy program 14, 15
   capacity-building 2, 15, 18, 68
   literacy development 15, 37, 39
   literacy tasks 16
   student engagement 13, 17, 43, 85; *see also* engagement
drama strategies 30, 44, 97, 116, 153

educational drama 85, 92
elements of drama 51, 75, 120, 122
empathy 11, 79
empowerment 8, 19, 90, 120, 138
engagement 15, 81, 86, 88, 89–91, 93, 117, 139, 157
English as an additional language (EAL) 13, 85–106
  academic English 86, 92
  conversational English 86, 92
English *see* literacy and language learning
experience 2, 5, 50, 67, 75, 76, 160
  experiential learning 67, 71
exploratory talk 96

facilitation 50, 120
Fair Go Project 85, 93
  big 'E' engagement 89
  insider classroom processes 90
  Pedagogy in Practice Research Group 86
  Priority Schools Funding Program 86
  small 'e' engagement 89
filmmaking 4–9, 157
  film pedagogy 4
  mobile devices 157
focused interaction 151
framing 153
Freire, Paulo 129–146
  beings of praxis 140
  co-intentional education 137
  compound codifications 135
  conscientização 131, 135, 137, 142
  dialogical education 140
  intersubjective dialogue 138
  naming 139
  problem-posing questions 136
  teacher-student contradiction 129

globalisation 61

Heathcote, Dorothy 129–146
  in-role 143
  role conventions 135, 143
  teacher in role 131, 142, 144

imagination 61, 63, 70, 73–75
imagined relationship 57
improvisation 71, 76, 78, 139
Indigenous students 40, 92
  Indigenous experience 59
inductive learning 132
information and communication technology *see* technology
inner talk 87
interplay *see* metaxis
intersubjective dialogue 138, 140
interventionist teaching 116

knowledge 27, 51, 56, 62, 91, 101, 113, 123, 137

learning ecology 50, 61
  ecological change 52
literacy and language learning 11, 30, 58, 92, 125
  emotional literacy 153
  outcomes 26, 27, 37
low SES students *see* socio-economic status

metaphoric transformation 74
metaxis 77, 99, 105
  liminal period 78
  liminal transformation 78
multiliteracy 70
multimodal texts 12, 17, 157

narrative 2
  narrative schema 3, 9
NSW Quality Teaching Model 93, 144

Index

pedagogical approaches 12, 86, 110
  creative pedagogy 15
  critical pedagogy 16
  dramaturg 124
  pedagogical reforms 68
  primary teachers 26, 29
  problematisation 124, 142
  transmission pedagogy 129, 133, 138
perception 2, 60, 73
place 91, 102
playbuilding 67–81
  integration of technology 153
  playbuilding pedagogy 69
playwriting 109, 110–126
  Aristotelian model 110
  closed approach 111
  flow channel 118
  Freytag's pyramid 110
  global view 120
  Muse 116
  negative instruction 116
  noble savage 114
  open approach 111
process drama 25, 29, 134
professional learning 7, 8, 14, 28, 29, 43
  co-mentoring 29, 44

ritual learning 53
role conventions 132

Sartre, Jean-Paul 5
School Drama program 27
  benchmarking 31, 43
  drama strategies *see* drama strategies
  funding 43
  professional learning 36
  student literacy 39
  timeframe 42
setting 3
social connectivity 12
socialisation 16
  social learning 52
  social networking 162
soundscape 156, 161
storytelling 2
  digital storytelling 157
super-dramatists 73
socio-economic status 85, 88, 92, 101
Sydney Theatre Company 27, 31, 45
  teaching artists 41

teacher professional learning *see* professional learning
technology 149, 153
  educational technology 150
  mobile media 153, 163
  mobile telephone 149
theatre literacy 121, 125
  theatrical codes 123
thought-language-context 129, 139, 141
transformative learning 63

University of Western Sydney 86

voice 91, 103

www.ingramcontent.com/pod-product-compliance
Lightning Source LLC
Chambersburg PA
CBHW050110170426
43198CB00014B/2518